MIND ODYSSEY

SPYROS PAPAPETROPOULOS, MD, PHD

MIND ODYSSEY

A DOCTOR'S GUIDE

TO TRAINING YOUR BRAIN

FOR PURPOSE, BALANCE, AND FULFILLMENT

Advantage | Books

Published by Advantage Books, Charleston, South Carolina.
An imprint of Advantage Media.

Printed in the United States of America.

10 9 8 7 6 5 4 3 2 1

ISBN: 979-8-89188-246-1 (Paperback)
ISBN: 979-8-89188-247-8 (eBook)

Library of Congress Control Number: 2025916105

Cover design by Matthew Morse.
Layout design by David Taylor.

08-21-2025 12:19

To my wife, Karina, and my parents, Mary and Theodore.

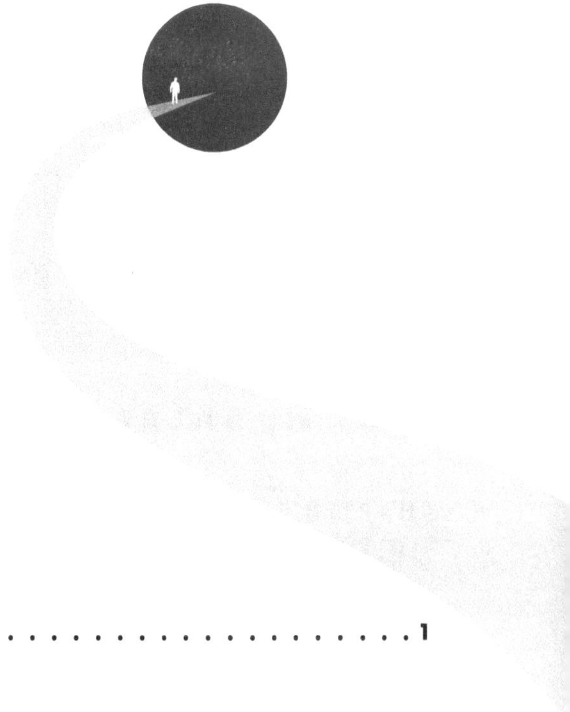

CONTENTS

INTRODUCTION

I was only sixteen, and I had to choose the direction I'd take for my future career. At the time, I was a successful amateur tennis player with an aspiration of going pro. Sixteen is about the age you have to decide how seriously you're going to take a sport like that. Players usually hit the circuit around seventeen or eighteen and often reach their peak in their early twenties. If I was going to make a career out of tennis, I had to commit now.

I loved the sport, but I had reason to be skeptical of that choice. To begin with, while I was undoubtedly talented, I wasn't even ranked number one at my club. Granted, we had some very impressive young professionals training there, but still, that fact said something about my prospects. In fact, as I looked around, I noticed a number of signs that suggested I would fall short of my overall ambitions—in particular, it seemed like everyone around me already knew the limits of my potential. As I thought over my options, I realized that, far from becoming the next Pete Sampras, sooner or later, best case scenario, I would become another tennis coach living off a brief professional career.

Ultimately, though, it wasn't my prospects that proved the deciding factor in choosing my next step. Instead, the decision came from inside. Deep down, I didn't believe in myself. I was aware that I had the ability, but I just didn't want to spend the rest of my life "chasing the little yellow ball." Great players find their purpose in that act. Even at sixteen, I knew that wasn't the case for me.

But if I wasn't going to play tennis for the rest of my life, what was I going to do?

This forced me to have some very deep conversations with myself. What did I want to do with my life? What was I even interested in besides tennis? What was I good at?

Many children at that age ask themselves these questions, but usually still in a hypothetical sense. Sixteen is an age for dreaming big dreams. I was making a hard, concrete choice.

With tennis off the table, I considered my interests. I had always enjoyed science, and I had some aptitude for it. Just as importantly, my parents were both doctors, and I could see how much the work meant to them. Like everyone else, they sometimes came home tired. They got frustrated by bureaucratic nonsense and annoying bosses. And they did their share of complaining. But at heart, there was always something to guide them through—a core purpose that helped them steady their emotions through the tough times and a sense of fulfillment from a good day's work.

No matter what happened, my parents knew that they could always go on treating and healing people. That knowledge anchored everything they did.

I didn't have any of that clarity for myself yet, but I knew I wanted those same qualities to be part of my own career. So that's where I turned. I focused on science and eventually became a doctor of the most fascinating human organ, the brain—a neurologist and neuroscientist in my own right.

In time, I would find those qualities I admired in my parents in my own work. I found my purpose, a sense of fulfillment, and the balance that would see me through all the tough decisions and major transitions in my career.

THREE CONCEPTS TO SEE YOU THROUGH ROUGH SEAS

I was born in Greece, so mythological metaphors come to mind easily. In particular, when considering the many successes and unexpected setbacks in the course of a career, I often turn to Odysseus. For this "man of many talents," the journey is full of incredible adventures that see him achieve unbelievable feats. It's equally full of tragedy and failure.

What ties the whole story together, though, is that Odysseus always knows his purpose. He knows why he continues on his journey across the Aegean Sea—in order to get back to his family. And that purpose allows him to see his destination: the place where he'll find true fulfillment. If he can just get back to his wife, Penelope, and son, Telemachus, on the island of Ithaca, he can know true contentment and success. These two qualities together give him a steadiness in the face of danger and setbacks. Through all the delays and misadventures, he remains balanced. Whether trapped in a cave by the Cyclops or facing the suitors who aim to kill him and take his wife and wealth, Odysseus keeps his head. While he feels intense emotions, he never lets them get the best of him. No matter what happens, he always steadies himself and turns his impressive wits toward his purpose and where his fulfillment resides.

Homer's epic poem has been foundational for many stories told ever since. These same elements—purpose, balance, and fulfillment—are equally important in a modern career as they were for a sailor in the tenth century BC.

Whether you're a salesperson, a software developer, a nurse practitioner, or a plumber, these same three qualities can allow you to guide your career through every trial ahead. They are so powerful because, in essence, they answer three key questions:

- Why do we do what we do?
- How are we going to do it?
- Where are we going?

Our *why* is our purpose. This is our drive, the engine that pushes us forward. Balance gives us our *how*. It's our ability to manage the inevitable turbulence that erupts from time to time over the course of a career. When we have balance, we're able to avoid overreacting to any situation—particularly negative ones. It's our coping mechanism for the ups and downs of life. Bad things are going to happen. They happened to Odysseus, and they will happen to you. Balance shows you how to keep your head and make the best choice.

When we have purpose and balance, we naturally steer toward our fulfillment. That's *where* we want to go. For Odysseus, it was toward his homecoming and the reunion with his family. This was the end of his journey. Because he had steady sailing through some very troubled waters and an unending drive to get there, he got home.

The same is possible for all of us in our chosen careers—but only if we have the right answers to those questions.

A TASK FOR STEADY WATERS

Without these qualities centered in your thinking in a conscious, well-articulated way, it's easy to find yourself at the mercy of the tide when difficult moments arise. You need guiding principles to see you through tough choices, critical junctures, and transitions in your career. Otherwise, you'll be at risk of going whichever way the tide takes you.

When faced, as I was at sixteen, with a fork in the road of your career, how will you decide which way to turn? Without a purpose, the emotional balance necessary to think clearly, or a sense of where you find fulfillment, you're likely to choose based on outside considerations: what others want for you, the job that pays better right now, or the way that's easier at the outset. These aren't unimportant considerations, but they are no way to determine the best career choice for you.

When you lose your job or miss out on a promotion, should you double down on your career or seek a new opportunity? When two companies in very different sectors both want to hire you, which should you choose? When you love the job but hate the boss, do you stick around? In each of these situations, the best way to ensure you make the right choice is having access to your purpose, sense of balance and fulfillment.

Ultimately, if you have a conscious understanding of these principles, you can—like Odysseus before you—keep a level head no matter what comes your way, choosing the best means of moving forward while always heading toward your goals.

Unfortunately, while we need these principles in tough times, we can only truly develop them when we have smooth sailing. And those are the moments we think about these principles the least. In good times, it's fine to drift a bit because we don't really need to worry about what we're doing or how we're getting through our days. When there's enough money in the bank and we're generally satisfied with our job, inertia tends to settle in. We turn our minds off a little bit and stop asking deeper questions because we don't require deeper answers. Like a sailor with the wind behind them on a calm sea, we set our ship moving in the right direction and relax a bit in the sun.

It's only when our situation gets more difficult—when the company is on shaky ground, when our terrible boss starts singling us out for the team's failures, or when we simply burn out and need a new challenge—that we realize we need to rely on these qualities. But these are the moments when we are not thinking clearly. Instead, we're living in a constant state of fight-or-flight, so focused on just making it through the storm without getting dragged down by the waves that we're frantically reaching out for anything that can keep us afloat. That's not the time to discover the purpose that really drives us or develop the tools to maintain a balanced perspective on life.

This creates something of a paradox: When we need the principles, we can't create them, and when we think of them the least, that's the time to do the necessary introspection to set them in place. I know that isn't welcome news to many of you who have probably picked up this book precisely because you're in the midst of a career crisis of one sort or another. The good news is that this book will provide some guidance to help you through the difficult period you're in. And once you're through it, you'll have all the tools you need to face the next crisis with your purpose, balance, and fulfillment already in place.

TRAIN YOUR BRAIN

The concepts in this book often feel ethereal. Words such as *purpose*, *balance*, and *fulfillment* are vague and hard to grasp fully—the perfect stuff for a fluffy self-help book. But that is not how they will be presented in this book. While I am fond of metaphors, mythology, and good stories—all of which will make appearances in the pages ahead—I've spent my career studying the brain. And every concept I bring up in this book is backed up by not just literary analogy but also hard science.

I'll dig into each of the concepts as they appear naturally in the book. Importantly, I'll keep this all at a very high level. The brain is our most complex instrument—in fact, it is the most complex instrument we've ever encountered. For that reason, we won't waste time getting into the precise medical explanations of brain functions that you'd find in a textbook. Instead, we'll stick to the main details that will help us ground these ideas in science and access the relevant parts of the brain most effectively. Like any machine, you can operate and train your brain better if you can grasp some of its operating principles. You can use this book as a brain training manual.

Here, in the introduction, I'll start by discussing a critical point for all that is ahead: It's never too late to change how your brain processes and perceives your work. In other words, if you've felt up until now that you lack purpose, your emotions bounce all over the place in difficult moments, and you have no clear sense of fulfillment, that's OK. Your brain can change that.

We know with relative certainty where in the brain your purpose, balance, and fulfillment reside. And we can access these regions through conscious effort. When using some basic tools correctly, the brain can be a willing partner and is very capable of adapting.

People think they cannot help reacting poorly to a bad meeting or panicking when facing a critical presentation. They feel they can't prevent imbalance in a crisis or a feeling of being lost when things go wrong. But that's not true. Achieving purpose, balance, and fulfillment is all about connecting the right neurons through the right synapses. In other words, you can train your brain to deal with negative situations and avoid the big dips or unnecessary highs that drag you and your career down.

In times of relative calmness, our brains are more receptive to making these new connections. This is why we have to be *out* of crisis to train our brains to behave better *in* moments of crisis.

The earlier you do this, the better you'll be at it. Time is our ultimate commodity. And there's no escaping that finding your purpose, in particular, takes time. But it's never too late. Whether you are training your brain to follow your purpose, find your balance, and seek fulfillment right out of college or near the end of your career, there's value in all that follows.

CURIOSITY IS THE KEY

To get much out of this book, you'll need to embrace curiosity. This is the curiosity of Odysseus, who strapped himself to a mast in order to hear the Sirens sing and who was even willing to go to the Underworld to learn what Achilles had to say about life.

I won't ask anything that taxing of you. But you will need to embrace personal reflection and be willing to dive deeply within yourself to find answers. There will be interactive elements ahead to guide these efforts.

By the end, if you engage in honest contemplation, you'll have clear principles you can use at any point in your professional life. No matter the nature of the turmoil you face, you will maintain a sense of direction and a balance to your emotions.

These same principles are likely to help you in your personal life—after all, resolving anxiety around your career likely reduces anxiety at home, and feeling purpose in your work likely helps in finding it elsewhere—but that isn't the focus of this book.

Instead, our priority is learning to manage our way through the storms we all encounter as we embark across the "wine-dark" waters of our careers. Some of those storms we can circumnavigate. Others we will have to expertly guide our way through. But none of us can avoid them entirely. With the ideas in this book, you'll be able to stand at the helm, confident you can face anything Poseidon could throw at you—just like Odysseus.

Δ

PART I: PURPOSE

CHAPTER 1

DEFINING PURPOSE

My best professional lessons have come out of moments of crisis. At its root, a crisis is often a test of principles. This was particularly true for one crisis I faced some years back. At the time, I was working for a large pharmaceutical company, where I was responsible for a team developing a drug for a devastating neurodegenerative disease that runs in families. We'd had some very promising early results, and expectations were high as we entered the human clinical trial phase. For those of you who don't know, the journey of a drug from concept to the pharmacy shelf is about fifteen years. At that point, we were ten years in.

Up to that point, all signs had been good, and the entire team felt confident we might have finally found a real breakthrough. I was as excited as anyone. After all, this was the work that really excited me: the potential to help people with a neurodegenerative disease, who really needed better medicine. If the remaining trials were successful, we'd have a truly life-changing breakthrough for thousands of people who suffer from the disease.

The only person more excited was my boss—the head of our research unit. He had dedicated his entire career to becoming an expert on this disease. His passion and knowledge had attracted me to the job in the first place. Finally, it seemed like his hard work would be paying off.

Then, we hit a wall. The human clinical trials generated a ton of data, but none of it was positive. The drug simply didn't seem to work. In fact, the data was damning, showing that further testing and refinement were pointless.

While this happens all the time in drug development, it was a huge blow for everyone involved. My boss took it particularly poorly. He just couldn't accept failure after seemingly getting so close. He kept looking for something he could do to rescue the project through the data. He wanted to keep testing, hoping we could find some way to use this drug—or at least create a reasonable path forward.

That was a major misalignment with my purpose. Years earlier, I'd realized that what really drove me in my medical career was treating people. Whether that meant treating individual patients or developing drugs to treat thousands, it was that act of improving lives that kept me going.

At the same time, I loved the work I was doing. And there were numerous other projects I saw potential in. I still admired my boss, and there was a clear path forward for my career if I just kept my head down and didn't say anything.

It would have been easy to flounder. I might have found obscure reasons to keep working or given in to fear about where my next job would come from and just quietly continued with the work. Luckily, though, I had principles to fall back on. I knew my purpose. Although

I was hoping for the best outcome, deep down, I knew that continuing to test this drug—wasting time, giving false hope, and potentially doing harm—went directly against that purpose. That gave me real clarity. At that time and with the information I had at hand, I couldn't justify working on this project any longer. So, I left.

THE IMPORTANCE OF PURPOSE

Purpose is such a powerful guiding principle in the rough moments of a career because it's the meeting point of what we're good at, what drives and motivates us, and how we're perceived by others. In other words, purpose is more than a job or even an entire career—it's what gives that work meaning for you. There are thousands upon thousands of doctors in the world, but they don't all share the same purpose. Instead, there's a component of the work that speaks to them individually, that others recognize they excel at, and where they find particular value and skill.

I discovered my own purpose in medical school. While I'd been heading toward a medical career since the age of sixteen, up until that point, I'd been doing so because it had seemed a better choice than tennis. It was only in medical school that I realized I didn't just want to be a doctor; I found purpose in treating people. That was the side of medicine that I was most interested in. It was also the side where I showed the most talent.

That purpose has proven to be the thread that would hold my whole career together—from researcher to physician, academic physician, and industry researcher. All the way down the road to the biopharmaceutical industry executive position I now hold, my purpose has been a central touchstone. Whether I am physically treating individual patients or helping improve treatments for thousands or even millions of people, I have always made sure my job allows me to directly fulfill that purpose.

In every job, it's given me my why. And that's crucial because humans need a why. We're built for it. Scientists believe that they now understand, at least partly, how and where the human brain generates the sense of purpose. It lies in the prefrontal and frontal cortex. This is the area of the brain that makes us human. It's where we form our emotions, regulate our behavior, and solve complex problems. It's also where we process life decisions by combining and analyzing memories and experiences.

This makes sense because purpose is a uniquely human need. Animals that have significantly smaller frontal brain areas exist largely on instinct. If you'll allow an overly familiar metaphor, they have simpler programming in place. We still have these same programs in the brain: Our instinct for fight-or-flight, our ability to learn to walk, and our innate knowledge of how we breathe are all still fully installed. But above that is a vast, complicated layer of connectivity, much of which runs through that instrument of purpose at the front of our brain.

But unfortunately, many of us often set aside purpose as unimportant at a certain point in life. We may look for purpose as teenagers and during early adulthood, but once we settle into a career and have a family, our focus tends to turn to everyday concerns, such as promotions, bills, and vacation plans. Life feels like it's happening too quickly to stop and take stock of a principle that feels so unrelated to grocery lists and gym visits and the kids staying home with a sore throat.

But clearly, even if we *can* live without professional purpose, it's doing us harm to do so—and that's never more clear than in moments of professional crisis. When we have to make tough calls about our careers, that lack of purpose leaves us adrift, all while our mental reserves are being exhausted by running without purpose in the background.

Over the longer term, professional success requires purpose. We can't succeed without managing crises. They're inevitable in life. And purpose is key to handling those adversities.

CREATE THE CONDITIONS FOR INTROSPECTION

All of this sounds great to the people who already have a clearly defined sense of purpose, but most of you are likely still searching. It's not enough to have a vague sense of why you do what you do. You need clarity here. To achieve that clarity, you have to start by taking care of yourself.

As I laid out in the introduction, you need to explore purpose (as well as balance and fulfillment) when life is calm and you're in relatively good physical and mental health. If you aren't sure on this point, just try to think through a complex problem the next time you have the flu or you're under a really stressful deadline at work. For that matter, try to focus your mental energy on an unrelated topic when you are struggling financially. This is extremely difficult, to put it mildly. Essentially, to find your purpose, you need to put a lot of miles on your mental engine, and that means you need the engine to be in good working order.

The reason for this is that when we are in distress, our neuronal circuits are overwhelmed, and the amygdala takes control of our behaviors. The amygdala is the most primitive part of our brain, and it's where we experience fear, rage, stress, and anxiety. In those moments, the highway to the higher functions of the frontal lobe is cut off, and instincts take over. In other words, the part of our brain where we do our processing and logical thinking—the part where we fashion our sense of who we really are—is not open for business as usual. We have to make decisions in this state—sometimes, big decisions—but when we do, we make them while in a state of heightened emotion. Those emotional decisions are rarely deeply considered.

If you've just lost your job, you're desperate. Your thought process is governed by crisis management. Instinct and impulse take over. As you flail around, you seek refuge wherever you can get it. The neurons that would allow you to articulate your purpose and make crucial new neural connections aren't firing in those moments. All brain power is diverted to surviving this period. And the fear produced in such moments often leaves you grasping for any potential solution.

It's far better, then, whenever possible, to manage the crisis in the moment or attend to any health issues and then, once that is done, to do the work and think through those deeper choices. That doesn't mean you can't do a bit of this work in a crisis. Everyone has some sense of purpose. You probably have some idea of what you're curious about and what you're good at. Use that as a guiding point, but don't expect to be able to do the deeper work until life calms down a bit.

For me, I could only discover my purpose in medical school because my family's finances were secure and I was young and healthy. I had problems like anyone else, but none of them were existential. Looking back, I can see how few concrete, serious worries I had. These were the perfect conditions for introspection.

Such conditions, though, aren't enough on their own. When you are in calmer waters, you have to choose to dedicate time to discovering your purpose. Time is your most valuable resource. To use it well here, you need to free yourself of outside information. That means no screens. You can't just Google it or ask ChatGPT to formulate your purpose. Up front, you need time to just do some deep thinking.

We have a natural fear of boredom, which constantly sends us toward those phones in our pockets. But to find purpose, we have to start with an active, engaged, and distraction-free mind.

PASSION IS A CLUE, NOT A PURPOSE

Once you have the right conditions and the time to focus on purpose, you need to know what you're looking for. Importantly, purpose has to go deeper and be more personal than the impulses we all have in our work. Everyone works to make money, for instance. That isn't a purpose. Almost everyone enjoys gaining power as they move up in their career. Again, that's not a purpose.

A purpose states what you care about in your position that goes beyond those material interests. What do you care about that doesn't earn you money or make you powerful or famous?

The advice most people give when searching for such a purpose is some version of *follow your dreams* or *follow your passion*. There's some value to that idea—as we'll see in the next chapter, your passion and your dreams are important tools for developing and maintaining purpose—but it's overly simplistic.

The problem with fusing the ideas of passion and purpose is that they are very distinct things. While purpose can provide a consistent center to your work for an entire career, passion burns brightly and then dims or burns out entirely. In other words, passion is a finite resource. It is a state of constant stimulation, and for that reason, it exhausts itself.

We all know this, of course. All we have to do is consider our most passionate relationships. Those relationships start extremely hot, but after a few weeks or months, something happens. Either it all falls apart for one reason or another or the relationship evolves. When we fall passionately in love, that passion lights up our neurons and produces neurotransmitters. This feeling is so intense, it's almost like a psychiatric condition. You see someone in an idealized way that makes you literally incapable of seeing their flaws. You'll do the most illogical things because you can't perceive them or your relationship with them in the way the world sees them. Like euphoria, this is not a state you can maintain for the next forty years. It's not a state you build a life on.

The different outcomes of passionate relationships usually come down to whether there's a strong foundation for the relationship or not. If you and your romantic partner share the same interests, have similar histories, or really enjoy each other's company and conversation, you can build on that substance and maintain love. If that foundation is absent, the love tends to burn out.

The same is true of our passion in our work. Let's say you love music. This starts as a passionate love. And that's wonderful. I, too, love music deeply and have interacted with it throughout my life. Such a love may drive you to learn to play an instrument, join a band, or do some weekend DJing. But a purpose has to be something we build a career on. Can that love of music sustain you through difficult moments, setbacks, and the tough choices that make up a career?

Possibly, but to know for sure, we have to dig deeper by investigating that passion. What is it that you love about music? Do you love the industry? Do you love the camaraderie of a band? Do you love the way pop musicians can create and set style trends? Do you love the lifestyle of a traveling musician? Or is it perhaps the act of performing that you love? Or the creative expression? Or the ability to teach and share the value of music with others? Or is it the possibility of fame? Or fortune?

These questions help narrow down what actual qualities of music attract you. They suggest where those sturdier foundations may reside. After all, it's important to have clear thinking in this matter. Most musicians do not end up becoming famous or rich. Very few musicians will become like Beethoven or Paul McCartney. Most struggle just to get by. If you could never be a great and successful musician, would you still love music the same way?

In this context, passion is best understood as a place to look when searching for our purpose—a starting point where we can aim our curiosity. If you love the creative expression of music, you may also love creative expression in other spheres, from marketing to fashion design. If you love the camaraderie of fellow musicians, that purpose could follow you into a career in HR at a small company with a really great culture.

From a passionate love for music, you can begin to find the root purpose that can carry you through all the jobs in all the industries that will make up your career.

CONSIDER YOUR APTITUDES

Passion is not our only clue to the nature of our purpose. We can also consider our natural skills and aptitudes. They can be a source of new possible candidates for our purpose or serve as disqualifiers when considering our potential as we follow our passions.

Taking that second point first, careful consideration of my abilities has been an important way of limiting where I seek my purpose. After all, as I've already related, it didn't matter how much I loved tennis. It didn't make a difference that I put in all the effort, showed up for every practice, and gave everything in every match. I was never going to be skilled enough to be as successful as I wanted to be. The same is true for music. I adore music. I even DJed a bit in my youth to make a little extra cash. But I have no natural aptitude for it. During my childhood, I took a few piano lessons. However, after about a dozen sessions, my piano teacher approached my mother and confided in her that I would "never play the piano" and that she should "stop wasting time and money" on this activity. Although I had the passion for it, I lacked the necessary skillset to take it to the next level.

In other words, tennis and music were never going to be the purpose I could tie my career to.

However, I always had an aptitude for science and medicine. The concepts that many struggle with always came easily to me. I could handle the chemistry and biology required to understand the processes of the body and how various chemical compounds interact with our systems. While many feel daunted by all the knowledge a doctor has to absorb in school, I found all that studying exciting. I never doubted I could do it.

Combined with the passion I felt for medicine, this was a clear sign I was heading in the right direction for my purpose.

LOOK OUTSIDE

There's only so much we can do to understand ourselves. We'll always have gaps in how we perceive ourselves because we can only look from the inside out. At sixteen, I was initially convinced I had what it takes to be a professional tennis player. Looking back now, it's obvious how wrong I was, but I couldn't see it. It was only because I was open to outside criticism that the truth finally got in.

This is often the hardest step for people to take when determining their purpose. No one likes to be criticized or to hear they may not be as good at something as they'd hoped. There are so many stories of the steel-willed genius no one believes in until they prove everyone wrong. But such cases are very rare indeed. Often, if we are willing to open our eyes and our ears, we'll find that many people are trying to tell us how much potential we have, one way or another.

For me, this started with my mother. When I was considering my tennis career, she was the only person who told me directly that she felt I could do better for myself. She was the one who laid out the financial picture for me if I did anything but become a top-level pro. It was because of her that I first realized that if I fell short of the top of the professional tier, I was unlikely to be very satisfied with my career or my future income.

This was a bitter pill to swallow, but I needed to take it.

Once I started looking for further outside confirmation of my potential, I began to see clear signals. I realized my coach never talked to me about becoming the best player at our club. He had never suggested I could take my skills to the next level. I knew he'd had such conversations with others. The absence of that conversation with me spoke volumes.

And then there was the heckling. One time, when I was getting completely destroyed by another player—chasing balls left and right across the whole court—some of the fans in the stands started chanting, "Why don't you try track and field?"

Any one of these sources might have been wrong, but all of them? We shouldn't take all criticism to heart, but when those who know us best, who witness our efforts the most, and who mean the best for us offer advice, we should listen. In fact—as in the case with those hecklers—sometimes, we also need to listen to those who like us the least. They can be the ones most willing to tell us the straight truth.

That goes for seeking other potential areas for our purpose as well. My parents didn't just go around trying to crush my dreams;

they made a point of exposing me to potential careers. They set up numerous internships at the hospital and in labs. They weren't particularly concerned about me going into medicine; their aim was to expose me to a world outside of sports. Ultimately, they pushed me toward knowledge and curiosity. It was through those opportunities that I saw the first glimmer of what would become my purpose.

Our sense of self-perception is so easily deceived or short-circuited. We can convince ourselves of anything when left in isolation. We need these outside perspectives to open new doors and close those that aren't going to lead where we want to go.

At the same time, how others see us deeply affects how we interact with the world and how we see ourselves. If you see yourself as a writer but everyone else in your life sees you as an engineer, this conflict over your identity can erode your confidence and mental health over time. It can also limit your ability to advance in your career. Who wants to promote a writer whom everyone perceives as having a completely technical mind? Or an engineer who spends all their time thinking about their novel?

We've all been on projects where we felt we knew everything and should be in charge. But if we keep hearing criticism from the actual leader of the project, by the end, we feel either embattled or disheartened. We assume that either they've completely misjudged us or we've misjudged ourselves. Neither assumption will aid our career in the longer term.

To avoid that situation, we have to open ourselves to feedback—both for what we should do and what we should avoid doing. Unfortunately, this may require exposing ourselves to some negative experiences. The truth is, there's a lot of value in failure, as well as in anger and hostility. If we're open to these experiences, they can show us where we are going wrong as effectively as touching a hot stove.

Some time ago, my daughter was driving us home. During the entire trip, she refused to hear that she was driving too close to the edge of the road. I told her multiple times, but she just wouldn't accept the criticism. A short while later, she called me and told me she'd crashed into a tree. Luckily, she was OK. But it never would have happened if she'd been open to hearing what I was telling her.

We have to pursue purpose with that same openness. Others shouldn't determine our path, but there's value in letting them have their say.

BE BRUTALLY HONEST

If we combine all these elements—our passions and interests, our skills and aptitudes, and outside perspectives on both—we should be fairly close to finding our purpose. In order for this process to work, though, you have to ask a lot of questions, and you have to be brutally honest with yourself. Your purpose speaks to how you want to live your life and what you value in your career. Beyond the basic pleasures of making money and buying nice things, purpose explains where your joy comes from in work. It's the meeting point of your talents, interests, and identity. It is where all your brain's neuronal circuits come together and fire in harmony.

To find that point, you have to be honest. When you're trying to determine if you're driven by creative expression or scientific thinking, it does no good to ignore the truth—even if it isn't what you want to think about yourself.

There's nothing wrong with being more analytical than creative or having more talent for plumbing than for law. The sooner you can recognize these things about yourself, the sooner you can achieve balance in life and find fulfillment.

Consider the question of whether you're more altruistic or money focused. Everyone would like to say they are altruistic, but are you really? Taking the path of altruism in your career will only lead to fulfillment if that is how you really feel. If, on the other hand, you care more about a big paycheck, you need to understand that about yourself. Part of a purpose is that it's sustainable—can you make the amount you need to in order to live the life you want? This may seem a crass consideration, but it's extremely important. If in ten years, you're making $45,000 a year as a social worker when you want to be a millionaire, will you still feel that you're living your purpose?

Once you have some answers, check in with others. Do they see you the same way you see yourself? Then, allow their honest opinions to really sink in. If they contradict your own answers, you have to keep digging. Ask more people, and check back in with yourself. Eventually, those ideas will converge.

PUTTING PURPOSE INTO WORDS

I started down my career path before I knew my purpose. I was curious and had a sense I was skilled and interested in medicine. I knew I liked it. And I'd had some positive reinforcement on the subject from family and teachers. Since I was required to choose a career at sixteen, I chose that. But it was more than half a decade later before I could articulate why.

This is often how purpose presents itself. It starts as curiosity, a feeling, or an inclination. Many of you probably already have the raw materials of a purpose that remains unexpressed. You have a sense of where you excel or what interests you. You know others think you are good at one thing or another. It's part of how you've ended up where you are.

But for purpose to really be effective in our career, we have to take this instinct further—we need to be able to state our purpose in words. Putting purpose into words helps us think through the idea fully. It forces us to go through the entire mental exercise and do the deep, hard work of introspection with vigorous curiosity.

The more time you put into these thoughts, the clearer you become on each of the principles in this book, and that clarity allows you to reach for them and measure your actions by them when you need them. Words give you a concrete point you can return to when considering difficult moments.

You can write this purpose down, but you don't have to. Your purpose can simply be your invisible mental banner. The value is in finding the right words and in continuing to ask the crucial questions—primarily *what* and *why*—as you dig deeper and go beyond superficial answers.

If you're a lawyer, you likely had some reason to go into the field. But to find your purpose, you have to get beyond the easy answers. Let's say you love to litigate, and you're really good at it. You love being in court. Why? If you win a case, what do you love about it? If you lose, what do you still love? Do you love being a part of the justice system and fighting for what's right? Do you love the legal process? Do you love excelling at research and finding rarely cited case precedents? Or do you love the exposure a big case brings you?

Keep digging until you're down to the core elements of that love and ability.

Ask others the same questions. How do they perceive you when you're in court? What do they notice about you after you win or lose a case?

This is real work, but it's worth it. Because I knew my purpose, I didn't compromise my principles when I faced that controversy with the clinical trials. I remained balanced emotionally and avoided overreacting. I was able to consider my options, and because I kept a clear head, I even managed to turn my exit to my advantage. I took my positive recommendations and leveraged them into founding my own company. Within two years, my team developed a new drug that's still moving forward in clinical testing at the larger company that acquired us.

I went from crisis to even greater professional fulfillment and success. It would have all gone so much worse if I hadn't known my purpose.

CHAPTER 2

REFINING PURPOSE

As a CEO of a publicly traded company, I deal with BS every day. Every day. They should really put that on the job description. There's not a day I spend in the office that I don't have some kind of emergency that derails my schedule and short-term plans. Whether it's a personal liability concern, a question from finance, or employment challenges, something will arise. And the thing about being a CEO is that only the most intractable, exasperating problems hit my desk. So, a big part of my day *every day* is solving problems no one else can figure out.

I often come home mentally exhausted from untying Gordian knots—unfortunately, cutting through them tends to cause more problems in business. What relaxes me at the end of the day is knowing that I am doing something I care about deeply. My current role truly fulfills my purpose.

At the same time, I know that this isn't the only role in which that purpose can be fulfilled. After all, if this role as CEO doesn't work out, I can always do something else connected with that purpose. I could become a CEO at a private company developing similar neuropsychiatric therapies—or researching medical advances in a completely different space. I could become a board member at a pharmaceutical company or a consultant taking on clients with really ambitious visions for the future of public health. I could go back to being a professor or researcher again. Or I could go into private practice again.

On really tough days, I like to indulge in a particular vision. I imagine myself as a family doctor on a small island in Greece. The mornings are warm and bright, the sea always within earshot. Perhaps I'd buy one of those classic Greek homes with the whitewashed walls and blue windows that you see on Santorini, with a nice balcony that overlooks an Aegean Sea bay. I could even move to the island of Ithaca, the birthplace of my grandmother, like Odysseus.

I know that I could always do that, and I would be content. That word is key. I wouldn't always be happy, and I wouldn't always fulfill every passion or ambition, but I would be *content.* And contentment is a very precious commodity in life. I could throw everything else away, and I would still be content because I would still be fulfilling my purpose and taking care of the people I love.

I don't believe in quitting when things get tough, but there's real comfort in knowing there are so many ways I could do what matters most to me while still being able to provide for my family. Not every day is a great day, but I know that what I'm doing matters. And I know I could matter elsewhere.

TWO TRAJECTORIES

The comfort I receive from these musings is possible because I'm fully aware that my purpose leads directly to a sense of fulfillment that sticks with me in every job and through all my career ups and downs. Essentially, I know I'm walking a path that connects my purpose, emotional balance, and fulfillment. Not every career path offers that possibility.

In reality, we have two paths we can follow as we climb the mountain of our career. One of the paths builds directly on the foundational blocks we're covering in this book. The other follows the more common interests and impulses that people mistake for purpose. In the last chapter, I mentioned how following your passion can end up leading you astray. This is how it happens. People enter a career because of a hobby or a general interest. Because they like this type of work for one reason or another, they're motivated to continue pursuing it. It becomes a passion for the work. Then, when they achieve moments of success, they feel true happiness.

So, what's wrong with that? It all sounds pretty ideal on the surface. The problem with this "happiness trajectory" is that happiness is not a sustainable emotion. We constantly chase it, exhausting our reserves of passion and motivation. Then, we either fail to attain happiness and collapse into sadness, or we do achieve happiness, only to see it evaporate in a moment. Happiness is almost always short-lived and is almost always followed by a crash. Like a sugar high shortly after we get what we want, our energy plummets. At times, this can take us so low, we lose interest and passion entirely.

In other words, whether we succeed and enjoy a moment of happiness or fall short, we end up in the same place—lower than where we started. Setting *this brings me joy* as our central focus, then, can only lead to the kind of transient happiness we experience with alcohol, drugs, and short-term relationships.

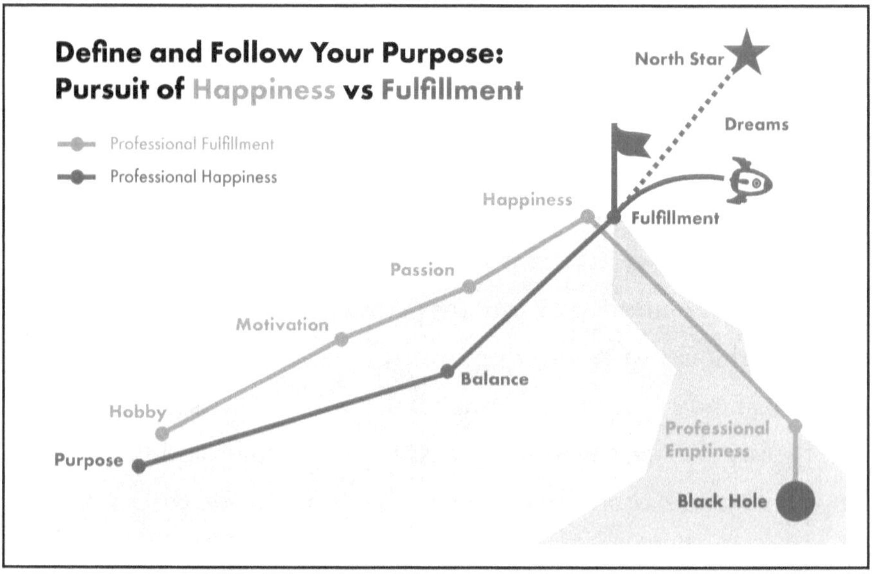

In contrast, the "fulfillment trajectory" uses purpose as its starting point. You'll notice in the image above that the path up the mountain starts lower than the happiness trajectory before running roughly parallel as we approach the peak. This is no coincidence. When following the fulfillment trajectory, we're on a path that shines a little less brightly day to day. Instead of relying entirely on those passions and interests as our sole source of deeper meaning in our work, we use them to fuel our rise. Underneath, we have firmer stuff that prevents us from crashing when we achieve success or miss out. This means we can keep going up without suffering major falls. This is the trajectory that makes room for rewards and accomplishments but can exist without them.

The spine of the fulfillment trajectory is the path we'll follow in this book, building from purpose to balance and fulfillment. Because purpose provides us with our foundation, it allows us to be level-headed in different moments instead of reacting emotionally. In the same way I can calm myself after a tough day, knowing there are many ways I can achieve fulfillment. Purpose gives us access to that crucial emotional balance when we're tired, discouraged, defeated, or facing difficult decisions. This "level balance" breeds further opportunities to train our brains to make the most of our time and harness our ambitions effectively. The combination of the two then makes it easier to find and maintain fulfillment.

This is a more consistent and sustainable path, one that can allow us to reach far greater heights.

DREAMS VERSUS THE NORTH STAR

You'll notice there's one concept I haven't addressed in that image: the North Star. Our North Star is our ultimate, unattainable ambition—the furthest extent to which our imagination can carry our purpose. For me, this might be curing Alzheimer's disease or developing a drug that prevents all neurological degeneration as we age. It's a point in the distance I can just make out, but somehow, no matter how much progress I make, it will always remain out of reach—at least for my generation, and possibly a few more after.

Even if I somehow attained one of those incredible, unbelievable goals, I wouldn't have achieved my North Star. Instead, it would shift, receding toward some other distant goal—perhaps developing a radical new treatment for some other neuropsychological condition.

Of course, I also have dreams, like everyone else. I occasionally dream of buying a nicer car and a bigger house—and maybe winning a Nobel Prize one day. Some of those dreams, particularly the last one, are also unlikely to come true, but can you see how my North

Star is an extension of my purpose, while my dreams are extensions of my passions? The former is focused on what happens outside of me—how my purpose could affect the world. The latter are all about what I get—a chance to enjoy a nice boost in happiness for a time.

Dreams are valuable, just like passions and motivations. They can help inspire our purpose and even refine and redirect it, as we'll see in chapter 4, but they aren't our ultimate aim. Dreams can usually be fulfilled, and achieving them or even just getting close to them gives us that extra juice to keep moving forward on what is most important.

The North Star, in contrast, is a point we're always steering toward. It's always untouchable. That's what allows it to provide our purpose with an ultimate direction, which keeps us fulfilled and balanced. In other words, this isn't something you expect to achieve; it's something you look up at from time to time to check your progress and the direction you're steering your career. In a perfect world, could the path you're on lead to that North Star? Or are you making choices that make progress toward it impossible?

This concept may seem useless on the surface—after all, you can aim for a house and buy it or aim for a promotion and receive it, but you can't actually reach the North Star you aim toward.

To address that, I'll refer to the example of a former Greek prime minister, Costas Simitis. He was fond of pointing the country toward a particular North Star. Everything he did was about modernizing Greece. Of course, you can never fully modernize something. As soon as you improve a system or add new technology, there will always be something more modern to aim for. The North Star always recedes into the distance, no matter how hard you chase it.

But that distant aim helped focus Greece's efforts in every area, whether it was infrastructure, integration with Europe, or social policies. Sadly, Simitis died in January 2025. But his focus on modernization remains his defining accomplishment. More than two decades since he left power, he remains known across Greece for that North Star.

CREATING HARMONY WITH YOUR PARALLEL PURPOSES

Having a clear North Star that is the ultimate extension of your purpose has value beyond your career. Knowing these two points also allows you to better balance the other purpose in your life: your personal purpose. This second form of purpose includes everything else that goes into your life—not just your family and friends but also your health, spirituality, and community.

Every one of us has this dual and parallel purpose. We all serve two masters. This book focuses on the purpose we attach to our career, but the two purposes will always be intricately tied together. After all, the more time you spend building a career, the less time you're at home with family. The further you advance in your career, the more resources you have to give your family. A setback at work will affect how you behave with your family, and vice versa. And if these two purposes ever come into conflict—if balance is lost and one suffers too much for the other—we will struggle to progress along any trajectory.

Therefore, we have to define, understand, and feed both of these purposes at the same time. I won't belabor the process for determining purpose in your personal life here—for most of us, it's fairly clear already. Any of you who have kids know how central they are to everything you do in life. That personal purpose will have as much individuality and complexity as a professional purpose, but here, the main consideration is whether you can keep your professional purpose (and North Star) in alignment with the purpose you feel at home.

Once you know both these purposes, you can seek points of connection that allow you to nourish them at the same time. To find these connecting points, consider the nature of the purpose you feel in life. For example, by nature, are you more a provider or a nurturer? Providers are those who focus on making sure everyone they care about has enough. That doesn't mean they're cold and unfeeling—just that more often than not, they're the ones focused on making money, building savings, increasing opportunities, and keeping home life stable and prosperous. Nurturers, on the other hand, focus more on emotional support. They do the bulk of the listening, the celebrating of big wins, and the helping of those they love through emotional highs and lows.

Personally, I'm more of a provider. I enjoy giving. I enjoy taking care of others. I don't need anything back in my personal life. At the same time, I have a bit of the nurturer in me as well. This works well for my career because I can focus on advancing in my work to better provide for my family, and I also do in my work the nurturing I do at home—either by caring for patients or by providing understanding to employees.

Passions and motivations can also provide points of connection. If you have a passion for creativity, it can feed into the work you focus on in the office, but you can also engage in it at home. Learn to play guitar in your free time or take drawing lessons—perhaps those skills can connect to work in some way in the future. I see this in my own life when it comes to my passion for health. Obviously, as a doctor, health is a passion I fulfill in my career. But I'm also a huge advocate for keeping your body and mind healthy in your daily life. For me, there should be no limit on what you spend to take care of yourself. Engaging in that passion in my personal life allows me to stay strong and energetic at work.

By finding these points of connection and monitoring the trajectories of your dual purposes, you can avoid most of the conflicts that appear over your time, attention, and energy. You'll know better where to allocate those resources to keep life moving in the right direction. This can only help in both areas. The more aligned both purposes are with one another, the more they can reinforce one another, improving the balance and fulfillment you take from them.

Ultimately, when we are on the fulfillment trajectory in our professional life, we end up with spare resources to attend more to our parallel purpose in our personal life. And the more energy and joy we take from that personal life, the more we can funnel into our professional life.

In those difficult moments in the office, when I'm dreaming about practicing medicine on an island in Greece, part of what gives me comfort is knowing my family will be there with me. I'll still be able to provide for them. Purpose in my work and providing for my family—that's all I really need. Once you see that clearly, it's easier to keep work and life moving smoothly along the best possible trajectory for both.

CHAPTER 3

PROTECTING PURPOSE

In academia, there are three big rewards every scholar aims for: having their work published in a prestigious journal, being funded for their work through respected grants, and promotions. As any academic will tell you, each of these goals is extremely difficult to accomplish. No matter your field, it's never easy to get an article published. This is challenging enough in new or less distinguished journals, but in the top publications, competition is particularly tough.

Getting your article into one of those top journals is so important because they have the highest impact factor—a metric determined by how many times a journal gets cited. Those citations provide the crucial recognition that most academics seek. On a certain level, that is the real reward for the efforts. However, to enjoy those rewards, you must have conducted research that is particularly impressive and insightful. Often, you also need a bit of luck or the right connections. Similar amounts of work and luck go into funding.

All of these goals are directly interconnected and can serve as stepping stones for each other. Those who get published and cited in prestigious journals are often at the top of the list for grants and other funding. And doing research that is published and receives grants often leads to promotions up the academic ladder.

These goals drive many of my colleagues. They envision getting published in a particularly impressive scientific journal and then being awarded a particularly large and prestigious grant. They imagine they will then be lavished with praise from the dean and the university president before receiving tenure and a top position in their department. To even have a chance at any of these rewards takes years of work. In my field, each project that might lead to an article can take five or even ten years.

That being the case, ask yourself what happens when a study a researcher has been working on for half a decade gets rejected by their first-choice journal. Importantly, once an article is rejected, the researcher has to disclose that information to other journals, making it even harder to get the article published in their second-choice journal, and so on.

You can imagine how deeply and overwhelmingly upsetting this would be. It could be enough to leave you questioning your entire career.

In an odd way, though, this can also happen with success. I've been lucky enough to have had articles published in a number of eminent journals. My work has been cited around thirteen thousand times. Before I left academia, I was the youngest associate professor at the University of Miami medical school. That is undeniably very gratifying. But after you get over the initial emotional high of that success, there's often another feeling that rises up—and it lasts far longer.

That feeling is … nothing. You get what you spent years aiming for, and once the sugar rush we discussed in the last chapter wears off, you just have an empty spot where happiness once resided. After all that effort, is that it? That short boost of joy—is that what it was all about?

There are many interviews with successful actors who mention having this same feeling. After spending years struggling to get on-screen, they finally land that big role that earns them fame, acclaim, and riches. They might even win an award for their performance. Suddenly, they have everything they dreamed of. People come up to them on the street and praise their work. They go home to a beautiful house in the Hollywood Hills. But once that initial rush wears off, they ask the same question: *Is this really it?*

Win or lose, when your primary motivation is some impulse toward a concrete improvement for yourself, you risk finding only disappointment at the end of the road. Either the event doesn't happen and you end up discouraged, or it does happen but doesn't live up to what you dreamed of for so long.

To exit this empty feeling, there are two clear paths forward. If you have fallen short of your ambition, you can give up and abandon your dreams. If you have succeeded and still feel let down, you can keep building toward something even bigger, hoping the next big achievement offers more lasting happiness. Now that you're published, you need the article cited a hundred times. Now that it's been cited, you need to turn the article into a book. Now that it's a book, you need that big research grant. Now that you have the grant, you have to become the leading expert in your space. Now that you're the expert, you can become head of your department. And so on and so on, forever.

The next win always has to be bigger. As with a drug, you never seek a smaller hit. This can work for a while, but as soon as you hit a bump in the road—as soon as you fall short of the next big goal—it can all come crashing down. As soon as that string of wins turns into a major loss, you're stuck with that empty feeling again. And it becomes all the more tempting to just walk away.

THE BLACK HOLE

The draw of following the happiness trajectory that I described in the last chapter—which follows a path of passions and motivations toward our dreams—over doing the tough work of creating a foundation of purpose is that the former immediately feeds our impulses. While purpose has a specific location in the most recently evolved parts of our brain, satisfying an impulse releases neurotransmitters—such as dopamine—that make us feel happiness. In other words, when a passion is engaged or a dream is achieved, our brains make us feel happy. And who doesn't like that?

When you get a promotion, when you receive a raise, when the size of your team expands, when you get more power over more people—these situations provide a little boost in the positive feelings that we all crave. Those impulses bypass purpose to immediately reach our animalistic programming. They speak to the basic rewards we all want for our actions. All mammals desire food, sex, praise, power, comfort, and so on. When we achieve positive career outcomes, our brains feel just as they would if we had secured food for our clan or become a tribal leader. This is natural and not something we should avoid. But those impulses also need to be kept in perspective.

When purpose is dominant in our career path, these impulses help support and reinforce that purpose—which then supports emotional balance and our sense of fulfillment. When we get the chance to make a presentation in front of the executive team, we experience positive emotions because it feeds our impulse that craves prestige. If that presentation is aligned with our purpose, we get that boost of pleasure while also staying on the fulfillment trajectory.

However, if we allow these rewards to be our guide—to be a substitute for purpose—our impulses tend to lead us off in the wrong direction, setting us on that happiness trajectory we saw in the last chapter. If we follow our hearts without a deeper purpose, these emotional impulses set us off chasing passions and motivations that we now know are unsustainable. Indeed, one of the neurotransmitters our brains release when we feel pleasure, dopamine, actually encourages us to try to repeat whatever activity initiated that pleasure in the first place. If we feel good after receiving a raise, dopamine encourages the brain to immediately chase that next promotion.

Even with a clear purpose, if we aren't careful, it's easy to slip off the fulfillment trajectory and begin defining success by the number and frequency of impulses we satisfy. And that means we're at risk of falling into a black hole.

The black hole ends up absorbing all the happiness and joy we should be experiencing in our work. No matter how well you do in your career, no win can ever be big enough to keep you satisfied. You can never become successful enough or rich enough or famous enough. Eventually, even achieving a major goal barely registers emotionally. Believe it or not, there are billionaires in the world who are truly, unbelievably miserable—and this is why.

For someone who runs on impulse, every win must almost immediately lead to another, bigger one. Every loss leads to complete devastation, and every situation has to be viewed as a zero-sum potential loss. Those stuck in an impulse black hole have to have all the praise, all the money, all the fame, and all the power. And it still won't be enough.

These individuals are strict for the sake of it. They keep wages low even when they can afford to pay more. They deny praise to anyone who has a breakthrough in their organization. They keep it all for themselves. And it still won't satisfy them.

You do not want to work for one of these people, but more importantly, you definitely don't want to be one of them. These black holes will suck in all of your energy, effort, and joy. They seek to spread their emptiness everywhere.

This may feel dramatic—and to be fair, it is the most exaggerated, if accurate, case—but this is the route we walk when we prioritize short-term gratification of impulses over long-term fulfillment. Once happiness and rewards become our focus and not just a benefit, we risk losing sight of the purpose that can leave us feeling fulfilled instead of empty.

SEEK IMPACT OVER IMPULSES

To ensure we are fully protecting our purpose, we need to understand thoroughly what counts as an impulse and what elements within ourselves we can rely on. We've already encountered impulses in one form. Our passions and motivations are long-term impulses that we can regularly dip into and satisfy. Here, I want to focus on the career-related impulses that offer a single, big boost in positive emotions. The list is fairly short:

- money
- power
- praise

There are, of course, other primal impulses we experience—the pleasure we feel from a great meal or sex, for instance—but the three impulses here share certain characteristics. They're all common forms of rewards in our work. When we receive them, they feel wonderful in the short term. And after that initial boost, we adapt and require another, bigger hit to get the same boost next time.

The amount of time we experience this emotional boost for is shorter than most of us realize. Think about the last time you got a raise. For a week or so, you were over the moon. You'd never had so much money. It's all you could ever hope for. Perhaps a week after that, you splurged on a car you wanted, put a down payment on that house you were eyeing, or booked a dream vacation. But then, gradually, you adjusted to that income level. Before you knew it, you felt you could really use a little more. Just one more raise, and you'd have enough to get everything you wanted. This is true even when your increase in income has kept well ahead of inflation.

This is known as hedonic adaptation, and it also follows us as we get more promotions and receive more recognition for our work. In my career, I felt a nice boost as I moved from junior faculty to faculty member, from faculty member to researcher at a pharmaceutical company, from researcher to executive, and so on. Each boost was really gratifying and pleasant. But within a few months, I would adjust. Even though I didn't consciously notice it, that dream position would end up feeling just like my previous job, and I would begin looking for that next big promotion.

The only escape from this is to enjoy these *impulses* while we prioritize the *impacts* of our actions. While an impulse focuses on the internal feelings of reward, an impact is external: It's about how our work acts upon others, whether those others are our colleagues, customers, family, society, or humanity at large.

Considering impact involves a higher-order way of thinking. It touches on how our actions connect to the world around us. In many social mammals, even the animal instinct is complicated by considerations of the impact they have on others. For instance, wolves choose to share a kill because they survive by living in a pack. The impulse to keep the food for themselves is tempered by the impact of providing for the pack. Dolphins, apes, elephants, and whales—all these animals show some ability to consider the impact of their actions on others and to prioritize it over their immediate impulses.

This external focus helps reorient us toward purpose, which connects to how our work influences not just our lives but also the world around us. By putting ourselves in other people's shoes—thinking about how our actions affect them and how they view us—we once again access that external element that allowed us to actually craft a purpose in the first place. We get out of our own minds and bodies and see ourselves through their eyes.

In the process, our actions become less about what we are *getting* and more about what we are *giving* others. If we keep our minds oriented in this way, impulses become nice rewards that help fuel the impact we have.

We find a balance between the perks that allow us to enjoy what we do and the impact that makes all the effort truly fulfilling and worthwhile. This fills in the black hole. While we will still always want more money, power, or acclaim, we don't *need* it to provide ourselves with a sense of worth. We don't have to judge ourselves by whether we've gotten that next boost of dopamine yet. We have a higher-order interest to judge ourselves by.

PURPOSE COMES WITH A SMILE

A big professional win is a wonderful thing, and I don't want to downplay its value here. Publishing an article in a celebrated journal, signing a big client, or launching a new product—these are fantastic accomplishments, as are all those promotions and raises. So long as you are grounded in purpose and further moored to the fulfillment trajectory through mindful attention to your impact, those wins are a nice bonus that can only help you on your career journey. They just shouldn't be your main objective. They're lovely incidentals—because your purpose is bigger than a single win or a single loss.

You might think this perspective could work against you in your career, dulling your motivation to go out and get that next big win. In my experience, the opposite is true. Prioritizing purpose and impact clarifies why you do the work you do, improving motivation in the long term. It also allows you to keep your own ambitions and impulses in context, helping inspire the people you need to keep moving forward. It may seem odd on the surface, but you can't have a purpose and be a jerk. Of course, we all have off days, but a person living their purpose can't consistently mistreat people. Because purpose is so intimately tied to impact, you are forced to consider other people and how your behavior impacts them.

I often talk about going to work with a smile on your face. But most of us can't smile knowing we are mistreating others to get our level of success. And I think we all know how much better it is to work for someone who has a smile on their face and who treats their team with fairness and respect.

For this reason, leading through purpose is actually more sustainable than leading through impulse. You end up with a better culture, better teams, and better people who are more motivated to see you and your company succeed. They'll come to you with problems and help you fix them. They'll stick around longer, even if they receive offers to work elsewhere. They may even join you in the purpose you establish within that team or organization. An impactful workplace is one that people want to join and work hard for. It feels good to work there. People want to work for you if they know there's something in it for them. If they know you think about them—that you care about the impact of your decisions on them—they're more likely to stick around and do more of the heavy lifting.

By default, then, you end up with a better working life and a better professional environment.

This is also, on a certain level, simply an easier path once you're on it. Which takes more energy: being thoughtful and impactful or being an impulsive jerk? I know that there's a side to all of us that wants to be a jerk at times. Wouldn't it be nice to always get what you want right away? But do you really want to be perceived by everyone as a jerk? After all, it's usually costly. It makes it harder to hold on to employees, as well as friends and family. It also makes it more difficult to get hold of and hold on to joy. Look under the surface of many jerks, and you'll see they are circling around an immense black hole.

Ultimately, it's those well-run, positive-culture teams that make progress for a company and the world. We may sometimes single out a jerk or two and claim they did all the work. But the people who really make big things happen are not the few jerks who put their names on everything but all the impactful individuals working well together.

CHAPTER 4

EVOLVING PURPOSE

When I was a neurology professor, for a long time, I wouldn't pick up the phone when pharmaceutical companies called. I knew they intended to offer me a position on one of their research teams, but I was content in my work at the university. I felt fulfilled in my purpose and believed my career was advancing at a good pace.

Then, something shifted. There was no major event or revelation, but one day, when a recruiter called to offer me one of those positions, I picked up. I felt intrigued, and I mulled over the offer. I hadn't picked up the first call or the second or the third, but once I'd picked up that call, I picked up the next and the next.

I realized that I had to reconsider my purpose once more. That didn't mean I had to start all over—I knew I still cared deeply about treating people—but I did have to evolve that purpose to reflect where I was in my career. My goals were shifting, and my purpose would have to shift along with them. I'd already gone through this process when I went from working directly with patients to working as an academic. Treating people stopped being about taking care of individual patients and instead became about teaching the next generation of doctors to treat thousands of patients. Essentially, I started treating people by teaching others to treat people. If I was so interested in these pharma jobs, what did that say about my purpose? How could I treat people there?

After some deep thought, I realized that my purpose could include treating people by developing impactful new medicines for neurological conditions such as Parkinson's disease. This dovetailed nicely with my evolving personal purpose. With a young and growing family, I felt a conscious need to provide more for them. I could make more money in the pharmaceutical world than in the academic world. That hadn't mattered so much a few years earlier, but as I was heading toward forty, it started to feel very important. Since my purpose could accommodate all these changes, the choice was obvious. Not only should I take the calls; I should start taking the positions and offers more seriously.

Eventually, I found a job that was the right fit. Once I was in the pharmaceutical world, my purpose didn't remain stagnant. It continued to evolve. It went from developing drugs to treat a specific neurological condition to exploring treatments across a spectrum of conditions. From there, it evolved into treating people with these conditions through executive leadership.

These days, I'm looking more at how to treat people outside of neurology and psychiatry. Once again, my purpose is evolving in real time.

I've been told many times that I've changed jobs too often and that I seem to be all over the map with my ambitions. From my perspective, though, they're completely wrong. Every step in my career has been clearly aligned with my purpose. The purpose didn't change; it just evolved to meet my new circumstances, opportunities, interests, and desires.

Everything I've done has been related to that original purpose of treating people. But now, my purpose isn't quite as simple as those two words. What started as a straightforward, one-to-one connection between my purpose (treating people) and a single position (being a doctor) has gained a lot of nuance and complexity that shifts with my life. That shift is no accident; it's by design. Because my purpose evolves, it never becomes outdated. I still feel it as concretely as I did at the beginning of my career.

HOW PURPOSE EVOLVES

Your purpose is like a living, breathing part of you. It has to grow and change with you. You have to take care of it and nurture it. As you change through the years, your purpose has to take part in that same change process. Otherwise, it dies—it becomes useless. If your purpose fails to evolve with you, one day, you'll wake up, punch the clock, and realize you no longer feel the fulfillment or balance you once did. You're just getting through your days like you did before you had a purpose. At that point, all you have to rely on are those passions and impulses to keep you going—a precarious path to follow, as we now know.

That means you can't just set your purpose down today, keep an eye on how you relate to your passions and impulses, and then forget about it. If you don't allow your purpose to shift and develop with you, you risk becoming numb to your purpose as the rest of your life leaves it behind.

To avoid that future, you have to regularly inspect your purpose to double-check that it accurately reflects where you are today. Once again, you have to approach this with open curiosity. Ask yourself if the words that you've put down for your purpose still ring true. Do you still feel the same when you think of your purpose or when you act with it in mind in your work? When you face one of those tough career moments, does your purpose help you remain emotionally balanced and calm? Is work fulfilling because it's attached to that purpose?

Alternatively, have you noticed that you tend to rely more on fulfilling passions or satisfying impulses to get through your days?

If some of your answers suggest your purpose is no longer doing its job, there's no need to panic. While it's possible to lose purpose entirely (we'll cover this phenomenon in the final chapter), most of the time, it's a question of evolving it—taking the root of that purpose and allowing it to develop to meet your current circumstances.

As you seek the exact nature of this evolution, let that same curiosity be your guide. It was my curiosity about those positions at pharmaceutical companies that triggered my own purpose evolution. Turning that curiosity inward, I noticed how excited I was by the new challenge that job would offer and how the increase in pay would feed my passion as a provider for my family.

The more I thought about it, the more I saw the direct line from my initial purpose to the new purpose I felt. It was the same; it had just grown with me.

As you let curiosity take the lead, you can run through many of the same steps we used to find purpose in the first place. Consider your passions and interests—have they shifted? Can your purpose shift to accommodate them? Do those around you notice that your skills have improved in one area or another, making you better suited for a new kind of work? How can your purpose encapsulate that improvement?

Before locking in that new purpose, be sure to ask questions that look to the future as well. Will this new purpose lead to the kind of career you envision for yourself? How far could it take you? Will you be fulfilled living that purpose in your work every day—even when things go wrong? Will this new purpose nurture the passions and interests inside you that most need attention? Can you find value in the impact this purpose affords you?

Ask enough questions with enough open curiosity, and purpose tends to present itself in its new form.

A SEAWORTHY PURPOSE

These kinds of questions will help determine if this purpose is really "seaworthy" or not. Consider how Odysseus's purpose evolves in *The Odyssey*. At first, his purpose is to "get off this island with the nymph Calypso so I can get home." Later, it's impressing the Phaeacians so that they'll take care of him and send him on his way back home. When he finally gets to Ithaca, his home island, his purpose evolves into killing the suitors trying to steal his family and his land—all so he can stay home safely.

All along the way, the central component of his purpose remains unchanged. It just evolves to meet the moment in time.

The same has always been the case for me. When I left my last executive position at a pharmaceutical company to start my own business, I did so because I sensed that my purpose of treating people was expanding to focus on my interests in innovation and bridging science and business. I couldn't explore those components fully at a university or even at a large, publicly traded corporation.

My central purpose remained the same, it just adapted to my most recent deep and abiding interests and ambitions. It's very possible that one day, I'll lose interest in business. Maybe I'll just want something simpler in my life, getting back to basics as a doctor. Or maybe I'll feel I can do more good by returning to the academic world or helping run one of those big corporations again.

Those parts of my purpose will come and go and change as my life changes. But on my deathbed, I'm confident I'll still care about treating people, even if I no longer care about all the rest of it. That's the difference.

PURPOSE AND TECHNOLOGY

Before we leave behind purpose for our discussion on balance, I want to take a moment to touch on how purpose relates to technology. Or, more specifically, the role technology should play in finding and evolving purpose.

These days, it's common to build up the potential and power of AI. AI is undeniably a wonder of modern technology, with many potential uses, but I feel that in discussing this breakthrough, we sometimes degrade the power and importance of our individual human capabilities. Human intelligence uses our biological hardware of neurons and synapses and their underlying matrix of connections. The code is unknown—because it's a lot more intricate than the algorithms designed for AI. It's based on a set of chemicals and electrical currents, and as a whole, it is still the most complex thing known to man.

I mention all this because our human intelligence is what makes us who we are. And purpose is one of our foundational codes. If you think about it, we really have two layers of code that we use to process the world around us and our reaction to it. One was installed by evolution, and we come with it "out of the box." This is our survival code. It includes our ability to breathe, our fight-or-flight instinct, and those impulses we covered in the last chapter. We have very limited ability to access and change this code. The layer above this, though, includes all the components that make up our individual personality, and our purpose is part of the core logic of this system. This is the layer that we code ourselves. Through outside influences and our internal, unique qualities, we shape it—and then it shapes us.

For that reason, we must be very careful about how we code ourselves. This is increasingly difficult in the modern world. Information plays a very important role in the formation of this code. Thanks to technology, though, we're now overwhelmed with information. The amount of data that a regular human consumes in a day is far more than we're meant to process. We now take in as much content in a day as someone would consume in an entire year a hundred years ago. Going further back, it's the amount of information someone might have encountered over an entire lifetime. Put it this way: A few generations ago, someone could read the same amount of information in the Sunday paper that their ancestors learned over decades. Today, we get that much information in a few hours online.

This information overload is more than just an inconvenient distraction—it affects how we think. Have you ever tried to make a really important point to someone in a restaurant when music is playing loudly and everyone around you is talking at a high volume? It's difficult to block out the outside noise and concentrate on what you want to say. Technology has the same impact when we're trying to think deeply, including when thinking deeply about purpose.

This is why, when explaining how to find your purpose, I recommended getting away from screens. Those screens tend to fill our heads with noise. And when we're overwhelmed by noise, we get flustered and exasperated. We can't think straight. This limits our ability to think as much as being in survival mode. We simply can't make all the new neuronal connections we need or access all the brain pathways normally used to clearly establish our purpose.

That's not to say that technology in all its forms should be ignored. Information is valuable. It's another source we can consult when seeking purpose or evolving it. Like feedback, it's an outside source that can help us check our natural inclination to follow our passions and impulses. In that sense, there's nothing inherently wrong with using AI or social media as part of the process of finding, refining, and evolving purpose. But we can't let this information overwhelm us. Otherwise, we cede our coding to the whims of algorithms and the unending opinions of strangers.

Modern technology is a wonder, but we have to see it for what it is: a tool. It's a potential ally that allows us to understand and encounter more and better ideas once we have a sense of what we're looking for. All of which is to say, we have to recognize a simple and blunt fact: Technology—despite its near-infinite information—cannot define purpose for you. No prompt will allow AI to understand you the way you understand yourself, nor can any influencer solve the puzzle of what's happening in your own mind. Instead, we have to use those internal processes, even if they're slower and require more effort.

For what it's worth, the same warning applies to all forms of shared information, even books. There are thousands of professional development books. If you tried to read them all and follow all the advice within, you wouldn't get anywhere. It would be impossible to act in any way that would accord with all the advice you'd absorbed. To avoid that, you have to either find a few books that truly speak to you and trust them or create a foundational set of beliefs about business and then integrate new information into those beliefs.

In other words, you have to create those foundations yourself. You have to write your purpose code using your computational brain power, one way or another. There are no shortcuts. You can't simply copy and paste your purpose from any other source.

One of the main differences between AI and human intelligence is that our brains need time to work on their own. They need time to consider the information they've encountered. They need time to organize and think through the information that is useful. And they need to purge themselves of the information they can't use. They need to filter and process that vast amount of information so that it's all absorbed and sorted to our advantage. The coding, hardware action, and processing happen on a different timescale compared with AI.

If we give our brains time, they can do some incredibly creative and introspective work. Initially, this may require some discipline: setting aside time, consciously putting the phone away, and finding a location that ensures the time remains distraction-free. But after a while, this process becomes automatic. When I'm eating lunch, I stay off screens. These days, it feels like the only way to eat. It feels natural. I'd feel strange picking up my phone or even reading a book during that time. And as I eat, I allow my mind to process and think—to recover from the information overload it's been struggling with throughout the day so far.

Of course, I'm not perfect. Perhaps the best time of day to contemplate purpose is right when you wake up. A rested, fresh brain can work miracles if you put it in the right environment, before it's overwhelmed with information. This is why "shower thoughts" are often so interesting. Instead, I wake up and read the news first thing in the morning—a bad habit I'm still trying to break.

But whenever and however you do it, it's important to unplug for a bit from that AI-driven technology world and spend a little time engaging solely in human intelligence. Because, like it or not, that's what you're running on. And using that hardware is the only way to get to your purpose and maintain it.

Δ

PART II: BALANCE

Δ

CHAPTER 5

THE BALANCING ACT

Heading into 2025, my company was in line to receive a significant government grant to continue our research and drug testing. Because we thought we'd won the grant, we'd already decided how to spend those funds on our research.

In any normal year, I wouldn't have had to think about those grants again—at least not until it came time to reapply later in the year. We had planned our financial year with those funds in mind. All we should have had to do was spend them. But after a change in government in January 2025, funding was no longer available for our projects. Overnight, we saw millions of dollars disappear.

Many leaders in my field found themselves in this position at that same moment, and understandably, many went into panic mode. There was so much that was unknown. Were these grant freezes temporary or permanent? If they were unfrozen, would we still qualify? If we qualified, would we receive the same amount of funding or only a percentage of it? Did we need to submit a new proposal for each grant?

Nobody knew the answers to any of these questions.

Businesses hate this kind of uncertainty, and panic is the most natural emotion that comes up in such circumstances. The easiest thing to do would be to give in to that fight-or-flight instinct and flail around, making rash decisions in an effort to remove as much uncertainty as possible. If I had indulged in that feeling, I might have cut jobs immediately or reduced our investments in various projects. I could also have remained glued to the news 24-7, tracking every article that contained an update or even just a rumor of an update on this policy. I could then have frantically shifted strategy with every update.

Instead, I took the news in stride. I wasn't happy about it, of course. It created a lot of major headaches across our whole organization—a lot of additional BS for me to deal with. But I avoided the allure of panic and remained emotionally balanced, rationally thinking through the company's alternatives and making careful decisions about how we could pivot away from government grants for the short to medium term. That way, whether the government funding spigot was turned back on or not, the company and our research would be fine.

I didn't let the news affect my motivation or my focus on the company and our work. I methodically reached out to various investors to discuss additional investments. The path ahead would surely be more difficult than it would have been without the disruption, but because I chose not to panic (as well as rage and other unhelpful emotions), I was able to keep my eye on what mattered and the best solution to keep the company advancing.

THE VALUE OF BALANCE

No story explains the importance of emotional balance in leadership quite like *The Iliad.* The entire narrative is based on warriors who make poor decisions because they are reacting in an emotionally imbalanced way. It begins with the leader of the Greek forces, Agamemnon, insulting his greatest fighter, Achilles, because the latter has criticized the former publicly. Achilles then refuses to fight for half of the story because he's too busy feeling insulted. No one attempts to make a well-considered, balanced decision. It's all overheated emotion. The result is disastrous for the Greek forces, who previously looked set to finally win the Trojan War after nine long years. This emotional imbalance nearly costs the Greeks the entire war.

But I don't think we have to look to ancient literature to understand the value of emotional balance. After all, we all know how difficult it is to work with people who really lack that quality. No one wants to work with a reactive colleague whose effort on a project is determined by the side of the bed they rolled out of that day. No one wants a manager who blows up any time a report comes in an hour late or who drinks too much at the office party when celebrating a big sale. And no one wants a CEO who panics at the first sign of trouble or who makes rash decisions depending on how they feel that day.

No matter your position, emotional balance is important for maintaining good team rapport, and it's a crucial part of good leadership. If we want to keep our team invested, positive, and moving forward successfully, we need to bring balance to our environment.

But emotional balance isn't just good for creating a harmonious work environment. It also improves our critical thinking. We can't think clearly in moments of intense emotion. Those emotions redirect our neuronal circuits away from what really matters and put them in crisis mode. Whether that's the euphoria of success or the dejection of a major setback, we are cut off from accessing the entirety of our human intelligence computing power.

Emotional balance, then, allows the brain to function at its highest capacity even in moments of great difficulty or triumph. We can make the best decision in the moment because we aren't closing off any areas of the brain.

The balance I am talking about is not a synonym for numbness. Humans are driven by emotions, which are critical to our sense of being. I'm not suggesting you never feel intense emotions again. Instead, balance is closer to the concept of equilibrium. When you have balance, you still feel things. You still react to events. You just don't overreact. And you simply don't let those emotions overwhelm your ability to see a situation clearly.

You can feel the happiness of signing off on a big sale without letting the dopamine that floods your brain affect your decision-making when you meet the next client or assume easy future wins. You can feel upset and angry about losing your job without sending your brain into panicked fight-or-flight survival mode and taking the first job offer that comes up.

The key to achieving this balance is not *blocking* these emotions but *training your brain to reset* to its natural equilibrium after that initial burst of feeling. You feel your emotions without letting them control you and overwhelm you. By resetting to your ideal mental condition, you leave all your neural networks open and active. Essentially, you restore standard human brain operating conditions quickly, even as you experience the emotions. After all, although the brain is not a muscle, it behaves like one, and it gets stronger and better with training.

In a less technical sense, this is a bit like channeling your inner Odysseus. The hero of *The Odyssey* is most famous for being able to craft a clever strategy even under intense pressure. When trapped by the Cyclops Polyphemus and facing death, Odysseus keeps his head and plots an escape that involves blinding the Cyclops and hiding underneath the monster's flock of sheep. When his crew sails between two sea monsters, Scylla and Charybdis, he once again avoids panic and remembers the advice of the goddess Circe, steering closer to Scylla because he knows he'll lose fewer men that way.

Odysseus's brilliance, then, is not just in his ability to craft clever plans but to develop them and see them through even under great emotional distress.

Perhaps none of us will ever be quite that cool under pressure, but we can train our brain to focus on our best ideas and enact them in moments of strong emotion.

ONLY BALANCE IS SUSTAINABLE

Emotional balance is a crucial part of leadership because leaders have to make tough calls quickly, no matter how they feel. But it's also important because highly fraught situations occur regularly in business, and the only way to avoid depleting ourselves is to regularly recenter around that balance.

We all enjoy feeling happiness. We crave it because it releases those feel-good neurotransmitters that provide us with a sense of pleasure. In theory, we all wish we could feel happy forever. But that wish doesn't hold up to our actual neurochemical reality. As we've already seen with the happiness trajectory, a feeling of intense happiness will lead to either sadness or a demand for ever more intense experiences in a quest to reach that same happy high.

The reason for this is that happiness is produced by neurons secreting those neurotransmitters, and they simply can't secrete them forever. Over time, these neurons may exhaust themselves by making new connections that need more happy neurotransmitters to reach a certain happiness high. This is why we experience an emotional drop after a big high. To produce the same high, we then need even more dopamine to trigger or maintain that sense of happiness. And thus, we end up almost in an addiction spiral, seeking more and more stimuli that will raise those dopamine and serotonin levels. And when we fail to reach those ever-rising neurochemical levels, we crash hard.

This is not a sustainable model for contentment in life. In fact, over time, it means we experience less happiness than if we had avoided chasing that feeling in the first place. And if we give in to the chase, we risk ending up in a near-permanent emotional void. One of the unfortunate qualities of the human condition is that while we can't continually feel happy, our bodies and brains absolutely can continually feel sadness indefinitely. Even if we aren't naturally prone to feeling low, we can exhaust our brain's ability to sustain pleasure so much that we make it difficult for our brain to rebound from those lows. Eventually, life can have more lows than highs. And if we can't escape this sadness, it can eventually become depression or a similar mood disorder.

Even if we don't end up depressed, relying on ever bigger hits on the happiness trajectory to maintain our positive feelings can lead to indefinite high levels of stress and eventual burnout. Because we have to constantly strive for ever bigger achievements without any setbacks, we end up constantly drained, with smaller and smaller hits of happiness to build ourselves back up.

It is one of humanity's great ironies. If we spend our time chasing happiness, we will struggle to reach the happy highs we hit earlier in our careers. In this way, happiness is like romantic love. Our first love is incredible because we are creating never-before-experienced emotions. We are flooded with new neurotransmitters and are making brand-new neural connections. It's an electrifying experience. For this same reason, our first breakup is the most painful. It too is completely new.

The next person we love may be more compatible, and the experience may be richer, but as wonderful as it is, it's hard to ever hit those same highs again. To really reach that same electric level of happiness again, the love we experience requires some sort of escalating characteristic: a forbidden tryst; a long, difficult separation; or a new, intense level of desire. Often, people end up abandoning a relationship not because of any failing in compatibility but because it seems incapable of inducing the happiness highs they experienced before.

If we're not careful, we end up chasing the emotional spike of that first love forever, thus missing out on a deeper, more rewarding kind of love—the kind that creates sustainable, consistent joy in relationships. This is the love we base marriages and families on, but it's impossible to grasp if we just chase that elusive emotional spike we get from the initiation of a new romance.

Luckily, we can reset the threshold for happiness—and love—in our brains through increased balance. In the same way that purpose grounds us and keeps us on the path to fulfillment, balance allows us to return to an emotional baseline, not by limiting emotional intake but by changing our emotional processing by gradually training our brains. And that baseline can keep our neurotransmitters from exhausting themselves and requiring ever more intense stimuli.

QUESTION YOUR INSTINCTS

Before we discuss how we can train our brains for balance, I want to address a false path many of us are tempted to follow when regulating our emotions (as well as our ambitions and time, as we'll see in a moment). Along with follow your dreams, one of the most common pieces of advice offered professionally is to *trust your instincts*.

Our instincts serve an important purpose. They are the central component of those default settings we come with out of the box. And like impulse, instinct has its place in our thinking and behavior. In nature, when we have to make immediate decisions without time to consider our options, the absolute best choice is to rely on our innate instincts. Those same instincts protect us when we decide not to walk down a dark alley or when we look at the sky and sense a bad storm is coming.

And in certain inconsequential day-to-day choices, these instincts still offer an easy means of reaching a solution to dilemmas. When considering where to go for dinner, for instance, we can feel free to trust our instincts. But our instincts can be wrong when dealing with complex problems or the modern work environment. Overall, then, we shouldn't rely on them to guide our professional lives. They shouldn't play a prominent role in determining our purpose, and they definitely shouldn't be involved as determinants of balance.

Instinct often acts completely counter to balance. After all, when I found out our grant funding had been pulled, the instinctive response was panic, not pivoting to a carefully considered solution. To ensure we make balanced decisions, we have to train our brain to turn to creative and analytical thinking over instinctual responses.

Admittedly, this can take some time. After all, our instincts are hardwired into our brains. They are the default pathways our brains naturally follow when making any kind of decision under pressure. However, even when time is short for our decisions, we should aim to make *quick* decisions, not *hasty* ones. A hasty decision is made in a rush and relies entirely on instinct. A quick decision, in contrast, allows at least a beat for analysis to take place.

Every time you have to make a decision, recognize that fact and just take a breath. Even better, take five breaths. If you can, take five minutes. Those minutes could change your life. They might determine if you keep your job, or if you keep a crucial client. For instance, if you write an emotionally charged email, don't send it right away. Walk away for a few minutes and then reread it. You might be surprised how differently it reads when you regain your emotional balance. After a few minutes, your analytical neuronal pathways can start operating again. Often, the result is recognizing how insufficient your instincts were when drafting that email while emotionally charged.

TRAINING YOUR BRAIN

Balancing our emotions follows essentially the same process as considering that email we just discussed. To train our brains to rebalance themselves requires consistent effort and, above all else, awareness of our mental state. This training is almost a type of mindfulness, but it's different from just being present in the moment. Instead, it's an active effort to recognize when our brain allows itself to be controlled by an overwhelming set of emotions. After all, we can't know that we should walk away from that email unless we're aware our emotions are spiking.

Once we recognize our emotional imbalance, we should turn back to our purpose. This is one of the many reasons why purpose comes first in this book. We need purpose in order to train ourselves to remain balanced. Consider the story I told at the top of chapter 4, when as a relaxing technique, I imagined myself living a simpler but purposeful life on a Greek island. At the time, I focused on how that story showed the flexibility of purpose, but the same moment also demonstrates balance. A tough day leads to a buildup of stress and frustration. To avoid poorly considered decisions in such moments, I de-escalate the stress by returning to thoughts of my purpose. The work and the stress are worth it because I am fulfilling my purpose. And if necessary, I can pursue that purpose elsewhere. I have choices in my professional life.

In other words, when I feel overwhelmed by emotional exhaustion at work, focusing on the many ways I can fulfill my purpose allows me to calm those emotions. By turning to purpose, my brain can put the emotions to one side to think more clearly.

Some of us have a natural ability to recognize when our minds drift in this way and return to purpose and balance. For others, this process takes significant effort and practice. The key, though, is to remain vigilant when your emotions are spiking and having an effect on how you're thinking.

In such moments, allow yourself to feel the emotions before turning your thoughts back to your purpose. Take a little time to analyze your feelings and what produced those emotions. Ask yourself if you are feeling balanced and capable of clear decision-making at the moment. Try to be as detached as possible from your current feelings while you consider this. For instance, even if you feel like you're on top of the world after making the sale of your life, that doesn't mean you are in a position to think clearly. In such moments, your emotions are unbalancing your thinking as much as when you are feeling disappointed after missing out on a big promotion.

If you are not feeling balanced, dig deeper. Why do you feel the way you do? What led to that imbalance? How did you get into this situation? How did you achieve this goal or fall short? What led to success or failure?

These questions are designed to turn our thoughts inward and to detach our thinking from the emotions themselves. We often want to project our imbalance outward. Particularly when our imbalance comes from something going wrong, we want to attribute it to others. But that places the solution in someone else's hands while also stoking the emotions that overwhelm us. Instead, we have to recognize that these feelings are within us, and if we take responsibility for them, we can restore our own balance. This is how the famous Oracle of Delphi worked its wonders during ancient times—by simply giving the advice to turn inward for solutions instead of asking for help from the gods or relying on others.

This process also allows us to learn from the cause of our current imbalance. If this imbalance is the result of a mistake we made, we can admit the mistake instead of looking for the cause in others, and we can commit to avoiding it in the future and move forward.

As ever, it's important to dedicate some time to this, particularly early on in your training. Instead of jumping from one success to hunting for the next one, give your brain some downtime to filter and learn. By focusing on purpose and taking lessons from this recent event, your mind can cool off and make calmer decisions.

When you train your brain this way, failure becomes just as valuable as success—in some ways, it becomes even more valuable because you can often learn more from failure. Take the time to see where you made mistakes and where things went wrong. As you train your brain to rebalance, you'll find that you have less to be afraid of. Whether it's getting tough feedback from a colleague, missing out on a bonus, or even being let go from your company, those difficult moments allow you to practice your emotional balance and learn a lot about yourself and your work.

In time, this process will become automatic. It becomes the natural thing your brain does after an event that inspires strong emotions. At the same time, it becomes easier to handle the setbacks we all face in our career. This is why, when I got the news about losing our grants, I barely flinched. Over time, and through brain training, my resilience to bad news like that became very high.

As soon as I got the news, my mind immediately focused on my purpose. Could I still fulfill it in this position? Could I still find a way to see our projects through to completion? If so, there was no need for panic at all. I saw the path ahead clearly, so instead of flailing and wasting time, I got right to work.

Δ

CHAPTER 6

BALANCING AMBITION

I came into my first biotech job full of self-confidence and ambition. I was in my late thirties and fresh out of a successful stint as a medical school professor of neurology, where I'd proven myself to be a high-achieving all-star. I had moved up the ladder at my university faster than anyone in my department. I'd been regularly published and celebrated for my work. So, I assumed my career in my new field would follow a similar trajectory. I would be greeted as the all-star everyone knew I was, and I'd transition to my new field as seamlessly as I had transitioned between the courses I taught as an academic.

I had this professorial mindset that I knew all the answers—that I was *better* than everyone else on the team because I had been a professor. The best thing everyone could do was listen to me and do what I said. This was how I'd taught my students, and I assumed it was the best way to engage with my new team. After all, I was the expert on the disease we were studying. If everyone listened and followed my advice, we were sure to achieve the best results possible on our new drug trial.

Bursting with hubristic ambition, I didn't take any time to develop new skills that would enhance my performance in my new professional environment. I didn't consider whether this environment might require a different attitude or leadership approach. I wasn't interested in developing and evolving into this new role. Instead, my ambition told me that I not only deserved this role but also deserved to keep moving up just as quickly as I had in academia. I was entitled to that success.

As you can probably tell by now, I was setting myself up for disaster. Because I'd refused to consider the new skills and mindset I might need in this new role, I didn't know how to successfully act as part of a team. I'd always made all the decisions for my students. I was used to being listened to silently, not having my ideas challenged by equals. I wanted everyone to just do what I said when I handed out assignments. When I received pushback, I struggled to accept it. I struggled to accept that I was not there to teach; I was there to be taught and to eventually contribute after being trained in my new professional environment, which was very different from my previous one.

This created an unpleasant and unproductive team dynamic. Even though I had a lot of great people around me who showed remarkable patience, I failed to take advantage of their knowledge or experience. I thought I knew better. Behind my back, my team called me "Spicy Spyros." This wasn't a compliment. It referred to my hair-trigger temper and my habit of blowing up progress on projects by throwing bombs in every meeting.

The only thing that kept me anchored in that first position was my purpose. I knew I was in the right field and that I was driving toward my North Star. But my overweening ambition was still setting me up for failure because my priorities and behavior were completely out of balance. In other words, my unbalanced ambition was undermining my purpose and, most certainly, my performance.

In the end, our team's hypothesis was disproven, and the drug we were developing did not seem to have the potential we'd initially thought. The project eventually failed. This is a common occurrence in biotech, but this failure was a particular blow because this was the project I'd been recruited to lead. It covered the area I was a real super-expert in, where I'd established myself as a key opinion leader in academia. This project was the reason I had left my academic position. Next time, I wouldn't be able to rest so much on my expertise. I was lost and overwhelmed with emotion.

Afterward, the company offered me a reassignment to another project, studying a potential treatment for a different neurological disease. This was a good opportunity at a good company—a second chance to settle into my new field and learn the ropes. I could have taken the time to slow down and really develop my understanding of the industry, perhaps adapting to the leadership requirements of running a team instead of a classroom.

Taking that position would have been the right call. But my ambition wouldn't let me accept it. Despite my poor behavior on the first project, I felt I should be moving up already. So, I made a rash decision and took a job at another pharmaceutical company. This one was studying a disease I knew a bit better than the one the project on offer at my previous job involved. I wasn't a super-expert by any means, but I felt I still knew more than everyone else. And this new position offered me more money and a better title, so I felt like I was moving up again.

Taking the job caused a lot of upset. I had to move my whole family across the country at a time when my kids were settled in at their schools, and we had strong connections across Boston. But my ambition convinced me it was the right call.

After that nightmare move, I failed in that second job as well. The culprit was the same. My unbalanced ambition had alienated me from my first team, convinced me to quit a promising learning opportunity, and led me to completely ignore my personal purpose—all so I could fail a second time.

It was not my scientific knowledge and potential that failed me. I could have been very successful both times. But my emotions, my ambitions, and my lack of essential knowledge of biopharma professional conduct let me down and allowed me to distance myself from my purpose. That's why, when failure came, it violently disrupted my balance, not once but twice in a row.

AMBITION IS A TOOL

Like technology, passion, or financial compensation, ambition is a tool—a powerful one we need to utilize in pursuing our purpose. But when left unchecked, that same tool can drive us into poor decision-making as easily as emotional imbalance. This is exactly what happened in my first two biotech positions. I thought I was pursuing my purpose, but my ambition became so intense that it stopped working for my purpose and started acting against it.

As the nation that coined the term *hubris*, Greece produced mythology that is full of examples of characters failing to balance their ambitions and their purpose. Icarus famously failed to follow the advice of his father, Daedalus, who told him to fly neither too high nor too low. While Icarus's purpose was to escape the labyrinth and return home, his refusal to balance his ambition led to his destruction when he soared too close to the sun, which melted the wax in the wings his father had created for him. As he plunged into the sea, he completely failed to achieve that purpose.

Like Icarus, we face as much risk from too little ambition as too much. While too much ambition can destroy your purpose, too little can keep you from making any progress at all. Daedalus was concerned not just with the sun affecting Icarus's wings but also with the sea waves affecting them. We all know someone flying too close to the waves. These people are smart, talented, and capable, but they simply lack the ambition to put those skills to work. They fall into the water as surely as those whose ambition sends them flying too high.

Unfortunately, we only have so much control over our level of ambition. That level is somewhat engraved in our personality. For the most part, the quality is innate. There are gradations of ambition, and we all fit on the spectrum somewhere. We aren't necessarily born with a place on this spectrum, but early in life, we end up in our general placement, which will more or less remain static for a lifetime. Put another way, it's very hard to go from having no interest in promotions and leadership to being filled with an unquenching desire to run a company. We fluctuate a little in our ambitions, but it's a matter of degrees, not massive shifts.

Occasionally, this wiring can change later in life, but it usually requires a major life event. Some people do go from extremely ambitious to leaving that behind, or vice versa, but we usually associate this with some disruptive revelation of one sort or another. Perhaps an executive has a heart attack and realizes that becoming CEO isn't as important as enjoying the years they have left. Or a person discovers ambition when they have a child and realize they want to invest more time to raising their child and experiencing parenthood.

Barring these sorts of events, though, ambition remains relatively constant in each person. It's so innate within us that we usually know how ambitious we are without thinking too much about it. And it's fairly apparent where others fall on that ambition gradation. When we meet someone in a professional capacity, one of the first things we notice about them is how ambitious they are—are they cutthroat, laid back, or disengaged? Do they seem to be focused on climbing higher, no matter the cost? Are they a team player, or are they just going through the motions?

Whatever your level of ambition, though, you have to find balance in it. This is true for those whose lack of ambition holds them back, but for most of the readers of this book, the concern may be the opposite. Here's the reason I know this: A book about finding purpose, balance, and fulfillment in work is only going to appeal to those who care a great deal about their professional lives. For those who lack ambition, the professional side of life simply isn't that important or interesting. Regardless of purpose, their aim is to make enough money to support those parts of their lives that matter to them most.

Whether this is a wiser way to live or not is not important for us here. Since ambition is largely innate, if you are ambitious, you have to tame it and balance it. You can't just turn it off, even if you think that would make life more comfortable for you.

For all of us who count ourselves as ambitious, then, we have to guard against ambition holding us back instead of propelling us forward. The risk of leaving ambition unbalanced is that it not only alienates our colleagues but also makes it difficult to recognize our shortcomings, accept feedback, or see which path is best for our career and purpose. If you are always focused on the next promotion, the next raise, the big bonus, or the next big win, you will never take a step back and look at where you are right now and how to connect to your purpose or feel fulfilled. Everything is tied to how you get ahead, which, somewhat paradoxically, often means you stop getting ahead at all. Luckily, this can all change with brain training, using the methodology outlined in this book.

BE AMBITIOUS FOR YOUR PURPOSE

The first step to balancing ambition is to return our thoughts to our purpose. Much as we did in the last chapter, we occasionally need to take the time to consider if our ambition is allowing us to achieve our purpose or is hindering our progress.

As we do this, we may have to push past some initial instinctive feelings about the state of our career and material interests. Our natural instinct is always to seek more for ourselves, and ambition is one manifestation of this urge. We will always crave more money, more power, more prestige, and so on. Our instinct wants us to give in to our impulses because that will improve our likelihood of surviving. But we've already seen where this path leads. To short-circuit this pathway, we must ground our ambition in purpose to see a better way forward.

Unfortunately, the relationship between ambition and purpose is not always straightforward. In some professions, they are almost synonymous. Some of the people I admire most are public school teachers and police officers. There's a ladder of advancement in each profession, but it's short and hard to climb. The professionals in those areas are driven by purpose, and their ambition is to fulfill that purpose. They aspire to teach their students well, even when they run short of supplies. Or their ambition is to keep the streets safe for everyone in their town, even when that town is at the center of the opioid epidemic. They think about the progress of their career and their pay like everyone else, but that's largely secondary to their ambition to accomplish their purpose as far as possible.

But most of us have careers in which ambition and purpose are less obviously tied together. We don't approach our work with purpose directly in mind. Instead, we chart progress by how well our ambitions are satisfied—tying ambition to our instinctive drive to secure ever more resources for ourselves. We gauge success based on our upward mobility. Our ambition is to run the company, whatever the industry is or however it connects to our purpose. Or else, we are ambitious about making enough money to buy a nice sports car. In such cases, purpose is really in the back seat.

To keep ambition in check, we have to tie these concepts more closely together. You can aim to move up in your company while linking that advancement to better achieving your purpose. That way, purpose becomes a check on unchecked ambition.

By turning ambition toward purpose, we can better judge if our ambition is healthy or destructive. And we can better adjust to the needs of our role, even if those needs don't align with immediate advancement.

Finally, by tying ambition to purpose, we avoid the possibility of ambition turning all our successes to ashes. Runaway ambition can lead to never-ending dissatisfaction because we're never moving up fast enough or high enough. Much like living by impulse, we risk falling into the black hole in which nothing ever truly satisfies us. But purpose can right our trajectory before we careen off in that direction. So long as we keep looking down at the purpose GPS, we know if we're heading in the right direction, allowing us to put on the brakes and turn around if we're flying down the wrong road at top speed.

LEARN TO HANDLE CRITICISM

Aligning purpose and ambition can also allow us to open ourselves up to criticism. This was an issue I really struggled with for many years.

Whenever I faced tough feedback, I would completely lose control. I'm not exaggerating here. Whenever I received blunt criticism, I would come close to blacking out in rage. I would feel such intense embarrassment, my hands would shake. I would literally see red. Once I had the chance to respond, my voice would be loud and would tremble. Even if I remained silent, my entire body would show how combative and antagonistic I felt.

To fix this, I had to recognize that I had a problem. And that realization came from identifying that this reaction was harming my purpose. I needed to improve as a doctor, researcher, and leader in order to treat more people more effectively, and the best way to get better was to listen to and absorb criticism.

The next step required training myself to improve in this area—with significant help from others and some training courses. I started by being mindful of my feelings when I was facing criticism. I would watch myself and simply note my reactions as they surfaced. Initially, I couldn't control my emotions, so the best I could do was excuse myself from the room as soon as I felt those feelings rising. I'd remove myself from the situation until I had calmed down. Then, I'd return and listen to the feedback.

After listening as calmly as possible, I'd try to sort the information I could use from the comments that were critical without a foundation. I would filter out the advice that told me I couldn't do something or that sought to do me harm (by cutting down my confidence, for example). With those unhelpful ideas set aside, I could focus on the impactful guidance I had heard.

This had a remarkable effect on my work. It was like suddenly regaining my sense of hearing. This was when I first came to realize how my team saw me in my first biotech job. I could only see my failings as a leader when I allowed feedback from my team to get in.

Later, I made even greater advances in this area after I took more advanced training on how to handle difficult discussions. It was like identifying that the tennis shot that kept me from winning matches needed extra work (yes, I am still working on my backhand to this day). After seeing some early results, I doubled down on improving on this area of weakness. I learned to focus on hearing more of what was actually being said (as opposed to how I was interpreting what was being said) and getting more out of each conversation. Eventually, I got so good at handling these situations, I became adept at defusing tensions before they arose in the first place.

Learning to accept criticism was a long path for me; it required a lot of work and change. I could only take that path because I recognized my ambition was getting in the way of hearing useful feedback—and that was getting in the way of fulfilling my purpose.

BE CAREFUL HOW YOU COMPARE

An important aspect of ambition is comparison. This is really how we feed our ambition. We can only know if we're moving up fast enough in our organization by checking if we are moving faster than those around us—or those who came before us.

Comparison is an inevitable part of our social existence. It's built into our nature; it is as instinctive as breathing. We're not unique in this. Animals compare themselves to one another all the time, and they size each other up and change their behavior based on those comparisons. Dogs compare how loud they bark, for instance, as part of determining dominance.

So this is not something we should try to remove. In fact, comparison can be a useful ally in balancing ambition—but only if we employ it correctly. Ambition often leads us to think about the best-case scenario. When we give in to our ambitions, we picture ourselves running the world. We're the CEO of the company, and it's growing at an astounding rate. And we've just been interviewed by *Forbes* about our astounding success. This can be nice and motivating for our purpose, but it blinds us to the obstacles that are holding us back and the contingencies that make such a future less likely. Comparison can fill in these blind spots.

Through comparison, we can see where others stumbled as well as the strategies they used to overcome setbacks. We can create a more realistic picture of our potential success and prepare for what may be ahead.

But if we aren't careful, comparison can also drag down our confidence. We are constantly exposed to comparison in modern life. One of the reasons we have to find a better balance with technology is that we are driven to compare ourselves to others every waking hour. Every influencer builds their career on comparison. They have the house we want, the family we want, the body we want, the career we want, the fun-loving personality we want. When we indulge in this kind of comparison, we are mostly left feeling inadequate—like there must be something wrong with us that keeps us from the personified ideal our ambition sets for us.

To utilize comparison and avoid these risks, we once again have to train our brains. This time, our aim is to filter out some of these negative comparison qualities so that we can find the value in comparison that feeds our purpose and balances our ambition.

Here's how it works. I find myself scrolling on LinkedIn all the time. When I see someone I've met professionally who has had some astounding new success, the first voice in my head is usually my ambition. At this point, it's not being very helpful. Usually, the first question it asks is, *Why them and not me?* But if I can suppress that initial reaction, curiosity rises to the surface in its place. I move past that useless question and ask a whole other set of questions. What is it about this person's success that really intrigues me? Is it money? The fulfillment of their purpose? Power? Is this something I can achieve? Do I want to achieve it more than what I'm already achieving? Or am I just feeling plain jealousy?

These questions all drive me away from external focus and toward introspection, probing if there's something useful here that I can use. Sometimes, I realize I am just experiencing basic jealousy. They have something I like; I want it, even if it's unreasonable to try to get what they have and keep what I have. Recognizing that, it's easier to just move on. My ambition in this case is being channeled into an experience that is completely useless for me. So why waste any more thought on it?

Sometimes, though, there is a nugget—some achievement of theirs that speaks to my purpose or a tool they used to rise up that I could borrow. To distill this further, I ask more questions. If it's someone I know relatively well, I think about their personality. Was there something about them that allowed them to rise to this level? Do I have that quality, or could I cultivate it? If they have achieved something that aligns with my purpose, I ask myself if there's a way to pivot so that I could be doing similar work. Would that require that I give up on some of my current work? Would that be a good trade? When it seems reasonable to do so, I might even reach out to the person to see if I can learn from them directly.

By doing this exercise, I move beyond my immediate emotional spike of jealousy and become more conscientious about my thoughts and the value of my attention. Instead of seeing someone with something I want, I dissect how they got it and see if I can learn something from them.

I turn this comparison inward and focus on how I can get better. And that's definitely worth my time.

COMPARE WITH NEGATIVE RESULTS

Because ambition points us to a positive future, our natural tendency is to compare ourselves to successful individuals, not those who've failed. But seeing the mistakes others make is as valuable as noting the keys to their success.

When I read on LinkedIn about some great person—someone who is smart, kind, charismatic, and knows their stuff—who has just lost their job, my first thought is the obvious one. *Thank goodness it wasn't me.* This is just natural survival instinct talking. But it isn't very useful to anyone. So, I've trained myself to move beyond that first reaction. Once I clear it from my mind, I immediately jump to a new question: *Why?*

I dig into the analytics of what happened. While ambition usually leads me to rosy visions of the future, this negative comparison allows me to take my survival instincts—already turned on by the story itself—and focus them on what I can learn to reduce the chance that I'll be next. I know I want to avoid that future at all costs, and now, I'm extremely motivated to discover what I can do to improve my odds.

Once again, I turn to a series of questions as I dive into what happened. Am I displaying any of the same behaviors that put this person's career at risk? Am I making any similar mistakes in my strategy or leadership tactics?

Often, these reflections turn my thoughts away from myself and toward my team. Of course, I feel bad for the person who is experiencing this setback, but often, there is little I can do. However, I have far more power to help those struggling in similar ways on my team. And everyone benefits when we lift up those around us.

History is littered with leaders who lost their position because the weakest link failed. When a train crashes because the driver fell asleep, the manager who hired that driver is often the first to lose their job. When a company falls short of its sales targets, the weakest sellers lose their jobs, but often, the head of sales follows them out the door.

By focusing on learning from these moments of misfortune that I come across, I find new issues my team might be struggling with and new ways I can help them improve. Reaching out to someone to discuss where they're struggling is awkward. We instinctively want to turn away from failure—both when we are experiencing it and when others are. It's like wanting to avoid going to the doctor when we suspect we're sick. Some part of us thinks that if we ignore the problem, it'll just go away.

As a doctor, I can tell you that this is definitively not the case. Instead, we have to take or deliver some tough medicine sometimes. It allows us to grow, and it allows us to help others grow with us. And negative comparison is a great way to see what kind of medicine we might need—for ourselves or for our team.

GRATITUDE: THE ANTIDOTE FOR AMBITION

People rarely notice all the factors that go into their success. We naturally attribute our rise to our own efforts. We don't see the external elements that push us forward. This perspective only further empowers and centers our ambition. We wanted to rise up, and because we wanted to, we did. We exclude all the things that contributed to that rise—whether it was the financial support of relatives, the mentorship of a manager, or just getting a job at the right moment, when the economy was hot.

Effort and talent are important. I don't want to minimize those. You would not be where you are without those. But the idea that you are solely the product of those efforts is completely false. And that view skews your self-perception and augments your belief in your ultimate potential. When you see everything as the result of your efforts, your ambition sees no reason to ever shoot for anything but the highest possible bar of success.

This is where gratitude comes into play. Gratitude is an antidote to that sense within us that we can do everything ourselves. It forces us to look outside ourselves at those who can do things better and whose efforts and wisdom move us forward. It allows us to identify the contributors and their contributions to our success.

When we practice gratitude, we should even extend it to those who hold us back. We have to be grateful for the good and the bad that have happened in our professional career—because they are the reason we could end up where we are now.

I've learned so much from the mistakes I've made and from the actions of those who set me back. At times, these lessons have been even more powerful than those I learned in moments of success. They have allowed me to learn what not to do as much as what to do.

Gratitude also opens our eyes to the serendipity that comes with success. I use that word purposely instead of luck because I feel *serendipity* better encompasses the concept that success requires things coming together in just the right way. Let's say you intend to open a store. You've done everything right, including scouting out the best location where you know you'll get a lot of traffic from your target customers. You've negotiated the perfect price for rent. Then, some rezoning happens, and the location is no longer available.

Such things happen every day. Gratitude allows us to see that serendipity was on our side on our way up. It also allows us to see some negative possibilities in the future. Instead of ambition telling us we'll continue to rise, we can train our brain to consider all the ways the wheel can turn. We can run through the potential outcomes, even the ones we don't want to think about.

And we can use gratitude to train ourselves to look out for the next time serendipity might come our way. Serendipity then becomes yet another tool we use to achieve our purpose. We can aim to put ourselves in the best position for things to go our way while still accepting how the wheel turns when the time actually comes.

I've learned this in my own career. In my third biotech job, I finally balanced my ambition and generated gratitude. And that's when I finally started to find real success in the field. I came in with a willingness to learn and an acceptance that my ambition had let me down before. I was just grateful for the chance to make up for my previous mistakes. I took a position that was actually a move backward, but it allowed me to grow into the role, really learn the industry, and make the most of my team. From there, I rose quickly through the ranks.

More recently, I set up a new biotech company. The idea for this company was born in my head, and my ambition demands I should take full credit for it. But gratitude reminds me it wasn't just my idea. In the first place, I was in the right environment that provided the right inspiration.

At the same time, several people were central in turning this idea into a reality. A friend of mine, Anta, works as a venture capitalist, and it was her efforts that allowed me to tailor the idea so it would be attractive to investors. Sifis became the company's cofounder. His biotech company was dissolving at the time, and he was looking for a new challenge. He was a super-expert in the ideas I was contemplating focusing on—areas I was not an expert in. Once again, serendipity was on my side. My initial idea became much more mature, thanks to his involvement.

Then there was Matt, who not only contributed intellectually to the idea but also helped us to secure our first round of funding, and my brother, Andreas, who is also an expert and who came in to help us further. None of these people were paid up front for their efforts. Until we secured that funding, none of us made a cent off all that work. We were simply united by purpose and solid personal connections, always willing to hear and help each other out.

So how could I claim this was my success alone? The original idea may have been my baby, but I was definitely not a solo parent. Like raising a child, it took a village.

Any major achievement—whether it's the completion of a project, the launching of a company, or the rise of a single successful individual—is really the work of many people. We need people in our corner and things to fall our way. That's the only way success happens.

In my experience, nothing quiets an imbalanced level of ambition quite like accepting that fact. I still want this company to be a success, but I know ambition alone isn't going to make it so. I'll need others, and a handful of serendipity, to make it happen. And when I have contributors on my side, I know the odds of capturing a moment of serendipity become much higher.

CHAPTER 7

BALANCING TIME

I always know when my life is imbalanced in some way because I can feel it. My internal anxiety levels rise, and that manifests physically. Whether it's a tightness in the throat or chest, a feeling of butterflies in the stomach, or restlessness when trying to sleep, when my anxiety hits a certain level, my brain makes sure that my body lets me know it.

Of course, anxiety can develop for any number of reasons. Some people suffer from clinical anxiety, which often requires medication. Other, "healthier" forms of anxiety include worry that develops over a specific cause. I sometimes feel this kind of anxiety before doing press for my company, for instance. But the type of anxiety I'm talking about is neither clinical nor tied to a particular event. It's short-lived but ambiguous. There's just a sense that my balance is off somewhere.

Because I've trained my brain for balance, I know exactly what to do in such moments. I take a step back and revisit my purpose. Am I living that purpose professionally? Do I feel that my work aligns with my mission to treat people? Am I heading toward my North Star? Do I need to revisit and evolve that purpose?

If my purpose is in check, I move on to balance elsewhere in my life. Do I feel emotionally balanced? Do I feel my ambition is balanced? Am I accepting criticism, displaying gratitude, and making the right kinds of comparisons with others?

As I assess my answers, I look for external issues that are raising my anxiety levels. I try to qualify and quantify these problems. First of all, I consider whether they represent a problem at all. If there is a problem, can I fix it? If I can't fix it, can I live with it? To really consider the size of the issue, I ask myself if I'll remember worrying about it three months from now. If the answer is yes, I know I need to address it now.

To do this, I take some time. As I've recommended so many times in the book, I slow down, take a step back, and—in an emotionally balanced state—seek a solution to the problem that is causing my anxiety.

If the problem revolves around purpose, I go back to those thoughts about how I could fulfill my purpose elsewhere. I could always go back to treating individual patients. I could always go back to the academic world. If my company goes under someday, I could always take more positions on boards or do more consulting. Would I feel more purpose-driven and fulfilled in any of these positions?

Often, the answer is no. And even if it is yes, I won't do these things without significantly more thought and consideration. But it helps to know there are other options on the table. It reminds me to focus on what I can control.

If my purpose is in order, I look at my emotions and ambitions and make sure those are tied securely to my purpose. I focus on making sure those emotions and ambitions serve my purpose, first and foremost.

But to do any of this, I have to have the time. If I can't find the time to slow down and do this introspection, I can't understand the source of my anxiety or reduce it. No matter how loudly that anxiety alarm bell rings, I can't address my emotional balance until I find another type of balance: balance in my time.

APPRECIATE YOUR TIME

Time is our ultimate currency and the most precious commodity. At times, our days seem long but the years feel short. I cannot stress this enough. We often define wealth by the amount someone has in their bank account, but no one is rich if they are poor in time. This is a fact we all know on some level and something we all eventually learn on a deeper level—but when we're young, healthy, and focused on advancing in our careers, it doesn't compute; time feels like an infinite resource. So why not trade a little time in order to achieve another promotion ahead of schedule?

But every time we trade off time to give in to our instincts and feed our impulses, we have to recognize we're giving away something we can't get back. And that means we have less of that resource to put toward what really matters in our careers. When addressing an imbalance that I recognize due to a spike in my anxiety, I must spend some of that same currency. If I've allocated all of that currency to earning my next promotion, there's simply none left to spend on reducing my anxiety. The account is empty.

We make this mistake because we fail to recognize that there are two separate concepts of time at play: objective time and subjective time. Objective time includes the seconds on a clock, the days on a calendar, the rise and fall of the sun each day, and the passing of the seasons. This time moves at a consistent, steady pace (more or less, if we leave relativity to one side). Time passes, no matter what we do. It trickles away from us at a consistent speed that nothing can arrest. As the Greek philosopher Aristotle put it, "Time crumbles things, and everything grows old under the power of time."

Conceptually, we bunch all our ideas of time into this category, but we actually experience time subjectively. Time passes more quickly or more slowly depending on our mental state—particularly our emotional state.

This confusion may arise from the fact that perceiving time is a very complex process in our brains. It involves multiple parts of the brain working together. Part of the brain is responsible for our circadian rhythm. Like many other animals, we have a basic sense of time that tells us when it's morning and when it's night, and when we need to eat and sleep. But unlike other animals, we have a perception of time that also includes contributions from our brain cortex—which is where we do our higher-level processing—as well as the hippocampus, where we access memories.

We gradually learn to perceive time on this more evolved level. Young children, for instance, don't understand the passing of time. It's a skill that develops. And part of the development of that skill includes the linking of dopamine and time. Reward and motivation play a crucial role in how we sense time passing.

All of this comes together to create a sense that time flies when we're having fun. And when we are experiencing a bad moment, it often feels like time has slowed to a stop, even as we will it to fast-forward. We try to make time speed up in those moments so we can jump to a time when we are no longer distressed, sad, or exhausted. Imagine the length of a minute, which is relative. If you hold a plank for a minute it feels like a lot longer than watching a TV show or playing a card game for a minute.

In other words, the single most determinative factor in our subjective perception of time is our emotional state. And this means that once we're emotionally balanced, we are in a position to balance our relationship with time.

The only way we can truly use this resource well is by training ourselves to appreciate its nature. This process begins by simply taking stock of our time usage. Do we feel balanced or not? No matter our age, it's worth using our brain training techniques and taking a beat every now and then to slow down and consider whether we're spending down our time capital wisely. I like to repeat to myself an ancient Persian expression: "This too shall pass." The good moment you are in will fade away. Your good health will not last forever. Equally, the tough time you're living through will come to an end. However you're using your time right now, this moment, too, shall pass. The question is whether you're using the good and bad moments as effectively as you possibly can.

Whether we are allowing time to speed by in the good times or trying to push forward to get out of our distress, we are allowing our emotional state to set the pace at which we experience time passing. At least when we're having fun, our brains are establishing new connections and we are experiencing pleasure. This is a positive use of our time. Trying to fast-forward through difficult moments, though, means we use up time without having anything to show for it.

That's why, after we take stock of our time balance, we have to focus on *appreciating* time. This word is crucial. When we *appreciate* something, we try to make the most of it. This is far better framing for our ultimate currency than enjoying our time. If we focus on enjoying our time, we still feel the urge to speed through the tough moments. In that state of mind, we either waste time passively waiting for things to improve or, even worse, spend that time feeling stressed out and pessimistic.

Instead, we should try to always make that time useful and valuable. We can learn from the tough times and find good moments in the bad ones. And when the good times return, we'll be ready to make every moment count.

Ultimately, we want to spend as much time as possible feeling good and perceiving time as it actually passes. This requires appreciating time even as it's flying by as well as appreciating the good moments we're having. We need to pull back from life and recognize when we're healthy, energetic, and purposeful in our work and ask if we're using our time well.

The more unbalanced we are, the more our brains will focus on things that are not productive. If we are balanced emotionally and ambitiously, we can *gain* time simply by appreciating its presence. That's true whether we're feeling good and time is flying or we feel bad and wish it would move faster.

REAL TIME MANAGEMENT

Often, our attempts to appreciate time professionally are limited to implementing some basic time management processes in our workdays. We schedule our hours on a calendar and perhaps bring in a personal assistant to make sure that we get to where we need to go and that meetings run smoothly once we arrive.

That's a useful technique, but true time management requires more than that. After all, we can be where we're supposed to be every hour of the day, but if we aren't using that time well, we're just sitting in the right seat all the time without making any real progress. Think about it like this. You can schedule your work time so that you maximize the number of meetings you attend. And your team can structure those meetings so that they follow an efficient plan. But you can get almost nothing from those meetings if you are not present and engaged.

If we don't appreciate our time while we're in each meeting, all the value can blow right past us. And that's not something we can solve by adding more people or another calendar event to our process. Even if we have multiple personal assistants and fifty people under us trying to organize our time, much of it will still get wasted. It won't improve even if we add a chief of staff or a personal cook or increase the number of people running admin in our organization. This is a matter of concentration and motivation, and that's entirely internal.

To appreciate our time, then, we have to commit to active engagement with the event before us. That requires a balanced state of mind that is rooted in purpose and an active attempt to learn from and interact with those around us. If we focus on each task, though, and appreciate that we are spending down valuable time on the activity, we can achieve far more—and sometimes save time in the process.

We can see this quite often in soccer. It's fairly common for a team to snap into a focused state when they go down to ten players. Before, when they were evenly matched with the opposition, the players were sloppy and wasteful in their offense and defense. Once they're required to focus because they are at a disadvantage, they actually play better.

Often, the opposing team finds the game harder to win once the team with ten players has that advantage. Everyone locks in. They appreciate the time left in the game and make the most of every second.

LEARN TO SAY NO

To improve our focus and appreciate our time, we have to be more careful about where we're directing our attention. When a team goes down to ten players, those players have to be conscious of how often they sprint for the ball or dive in for a tackle. There's no room for waste. To continue to concentrate intensely, they have to avoid distractions and focus on doing what adds the most value to the team's efforts.

The same is true of time in our professional life. We have to focus on the work that matters most so that we don't waste our time and attention on work that others can do. That means we have to accept that we aren't there to do everyone else's work. We have to learn to say no sometimes, even if that upsets people.

Ultimately, a business can only work if each person does their part. One person has a project to complete, and another has a sales quota to hit. It's nice to do a favor or help pick up some of the extra load occasionally, but we have to set firm boundaries around these exceptions. Otherwise, we can drain all our resources, leaving too little to do the work that actually matters most in our position.

And the more we say yes when we should say no, the more people tend to assume they can keep asking. When we accept extra responsibilities, we might get a thank-you, but people internalize that they can push more work on us in the future. To avoid that, we have to start saying no to additional work.

In chapter 3, I mentioned that you can't be a jerk when you have a purpose, and that's still true. But that doesn't mean you have to be a pushover. Help where you can afford to help out, but you shouldn't feel you have to do more than you can justify with your time.

This is a particularly difficult lesson for entrepreneurs. Because it's their company, they feel a responsibility to pitch in everywhere. Early on, that may be necessary, but when the company is running smoothly, their time is best spent leading, not getting involved in every task.

Leaders also struggle with this because they want to lift up those who are falling behind. As I mentioned in the last chapter, it's good to learn from those who fail, see those who are at risk of failure in your organization, and give them a boost. But we have to set limits here. I've avoided the word *empathy* in this book because I feel it's a slippery term that gets overused. Often, when it gets employed, it's used as an excuse for breaking down the boundaries we try to put up. We are expected to feel such concern for others that we put them before ourselves and our responsibilities. This is not a good way to use our limited resources.

Once again, balance is required. We have to be balanced in our consideration of others. We need balance in the time we spend on our own work obligations and the time we spend on helping others when they fall behind.

At times, we can justify giving a little more, but we can't always tip the balance in favor of empathy. That policy will quickly lead us off course. We shouldn't ignore the needs of others, but we can't focus our time solely on pleasing them. Instead, we should aim to be fair—helping when we can afford to help and recognizing when it's time for someone to either rise or fall on their own.

REST ISN'T JUST FOR RETIREMENT

One of the greatest time imbalances in professional life is the amount we rest. We all crave downtime—the time we can spend playing, enjoying family, and experiencing new things. In an ideal world, we'd all have more downtime in our days, weeks, months, and years. But going against this sentiment is that we also want to have enough financial security to justify working less. Ironically, most of us chase that second instinct at the expense of the first, which leads us to spend even less time resting than we might have otherwise. We work longer hours, take work home on the weekends, and refuse to take the vacation days we're guaranteed in our contracts, all so we can get a little closer to that prized financial certainty.

We work so hard that when we finally do get a break at the end of the day, we waste our restful hours by staring at a screen. When we finally book a real vacation, we focus so much on filling those free hours that we barely take a moment to enjoy it.

We justify all of this by delaying rest until later. Someday, we'll take a few weeks off and visit Europe. Someday, we'll be in a position where we can guarantee that our weekends are free to spend time with the kids. The ultimate destination of our future resting time is retirement. Like Odysseus returning to Ithaca, we fantasize that all our hard work will pay off then. We'll have that long-sought financial certainty and years to enjoy our time.

But delaying rest creates an immense imbalance right now—all for a future that is far from guaranteed. We assume that our sacrifices will pay off in retirement, but any number of events can affect our plans. There may be a financial crisis that drains our savings, removing financial security. We may develop health issues that reduce our ability to make the most of that time. The years we plan to spend with family may not be possible if we don't build strong relationships while our children are young. And we may die. Even if things generally go as planned, it's very common for people to reach retirement only to discover they don't know what to do with all that time. They've filled so many of their hours with work that they haven't built up the interests and relationships to make that time count.

In other words, we could labor for decades, waiting to rest, and find no rest at the end of the journey.

I'm not advocating for quitting your job or spending all your retirement savings here. But it's important to state a fact that, deep down, we all know: Time matters most when we feel well and balanced.

It has the most value when we can do something with it. When we're healthy, our kids are young, and we have money in the bank, that's the time we should be focused on using rest. And this focus on delaying rest until retirement can lead us to waste our best years.

We must balance our need and desire to work for financial security and achieving our purpose while using our time wisely. And in both areas of our life, we should seek to maximize the quality of that time. That means less time on the screen at home and more focused time at work to get things done.

Time is a wonderful tool. It's our greatest resource. We should balance our use of it now, while we have the time. We'll get more from our time today, and often, that makes for a better retirement down the road.

TIME IS ALWAYS THE MORE VALUABLE RESOURCE

There's a story I've always loved about Aristotle Onassis. I don't know if it's apocryphal or not, but it's always spoken very deeply to my beliefs about time.

Onassis is no longer quite the big name he was during his life, but for a while in the 1970s, he was one of the faces of business success. A shipping magnate, he ended up marrying John F. Kennedy's glamorous widow, Jackie.

Despite his massive wealth and reputation for elegance, Onassis was born in a simple fishing village outside modern-day Izmir, Turkey (it was a Greek city called Smyrna back then). He remained fond of his home, and he would regularly visit fishing towns on Greek islands and sit down with the locals for a chat at one café or another.

On one such visit, Onassis found himself sitting across from a local fisherman who didn't recognize him. It was early afternoon, and the sea was visible from their seats in the café. Onassis, as he often did, began asking questions of the fisherman. Considering the time of day, he started by asking why the fisherman was at a café in the first place.

"It's a beautiful day, and the sea is full of fish. Why are you sitting here with me?" he asked.

The fisherman gave a pleasant chuckle. "What should I be doing?"

"Fishing, of course!"

With a gentle wave of his hand, the fisherman dismissed the idea entirely. "I did that for a few hours this morning and caught enough for the day."

"But you could be out there catching more," said Onassis, as his businessman's mind began to whirl. "You could catch enough that you would be able to hire some help. That would allow you to catch even more fish. Then, you could catch enough to buy another fishing boat and hire more help. Eventually, you could have a fleet of boats."

"And then what?"

"Listen," Onassis said, sitting back in his seat contentedly. "You may not know me … it's no matter. I'm very successful. So I can tell you, when you become successful like me, you have so much more time on your hands. Time when you can sit back and really enjoy your life."

"What are you talking about?" the fisherman said with another chuckle. "I could do all that work just so I could spend my time doing what I'm already doing?"

Our work is an important part of our lives. And most of us can't afford to duck out of the office at noon to enjoy a coffee and stare at the sea. But the fisherman's point isn't one we should be quick to dismiss. We are all very comfortable with the fact that we only have so many dollars in our account, and once we've spent them, there's no money left. With dollars, we can always work more and replenish our account, but that isn't true of the other currencies we spend. We spend some of our health currency every time we make an unhealthy decision. Smoking cigarettes, eating bad food, failing to work out—eventually, we spend down that currency we have in life, and we run out.

Like health, time is a currency we never get more of. And once we run out, it doesn't matter how many dollars we have in the bank.

All of which is to say, if we are going to spend so much of this currency on our work, we should make sure that it's purposeful as well as profitable. And we should make sure to balance our time while we're there.

PART III: FULFILLMENT

CHAPTER 8

CLEAR SAILING

I remember very vividly the first time the FDA approved a drug I had worked on. It was one of the most professionally fulfilling moments of my life. I was working at my second biotech company, and this was my first experience of the thrill of seeing all the hard work pay off and all the data come back positive from years of clinical trials.

The treatment involved an innovative use of Botox to treat chronic migraine. Our theory was that Botox could change the activity of the neurotransmitters that control pain—the same way it does in the face, which allows it to reduce wrinkles—thus avoiding cripplingly painful headaches. The approval of this treatment would be life-changing for potentially millions of people. And I had played a part in making that happen.

To be clear, the whole process required a huge team of brilliant scientists and managers, but I definitely had an important role. If bringing a treatment to market requires an army, I had been one of the generals—not the main general, but an important leader in the officer corps.

My outsized level of fulfillment compared to the size of my role was what surprised me most about the experience. I had done my part to move the treatment forward, but I felt fulfilled because of the treatment itself—because of the good we were going to do for people. I cared about the impact of the project. I barely noticed that the praise rarely centered on me.

I was incredibly proud when our work was featured in *TIME* as one of the top ten scientific breakthroughs of the year, even though my name wasn't mentioned in the article. In fact, other than the pride I felt, the breakthrough wasn't particularly significant for me or my career. I didn't get public credit. I didn't get rich when the treatment hit the market. The team knew the role I'd played, as did those who dug into the research, but my work was anonymous to the wider world.

But for the first time in my career, I didn't care. I could look back and see the value of the work I'd done. That meant far more to me than a cover story ever could. And that's why, for the first time, I felt like I really had a future in this field. I could see a world in which I could keep doing this and feeling purposeful and balanced for years to come.

These drug trials are so protracted that you can't coast along on wins. You can't hold out long enough for another guaranteed big hit of dopamine after another success. It's years of ups and downs, and you can spend those years working tirelessly, all for your treatment to fail through no fault of your own. Once again, there's a bit of serendipity involved. All the science can be in order, the theory can be sound, and the treatment will either move forward or not based on results that may simply be out of your hands.

Instead of aiming for those dopamine highs, then, the only real option is to view the whole process as a journey. And I realized in that moment that it was a journey I truly enjoyed being on.

Six months later, I had to change jobs and move my family again. Unlike the last time, though, this wasn't an impetuous, ambition-based decision. It was the right call. And even with that disruption, my feeling of fulfillment didn't lessen. As we left the sunny California coast that we'd all come to love for chilly Boston, I felt fully aligned in my purpose and balance. I was ready to tackle the new challenge.

There was a lot going wrong in my life at that time. Once again, my family struggled with the move. They didn't want to leave California, and neither did I for that matter. But I still felt energized professionally. I knew I had the qualities within myself to continue on this path, and even as I was struggling with all the changes, I couldn't wait for my next professional test.

A BETTER PARTNER THAN HAPPINESS

Fulfillment is where the whole process we've been learning has been leading. You can think of it as your reward for finding purpose and being balanced. It's a super balanced state—one in which we feel content and satisfied professionally, all while we increase our resilience to the tough moments in our career.

This isn't possible until we have a clearly defined purpose and achieve balance in our life. In a very real way, fulfillment emerges on its own from the combination of those two elements. It's a natural state we achieve when all the other pieces of the puzzle are in place. We know we're doing what we're supposed to be doing, we are focused on making an impact over chasing impulses, and we feel balanced in our emotions, our ambitions, and our appreciation of time. In this state, we can weather the tough moments and appreciate the good ones without huge shifts in our emotional state. And that allows us to consistently sail toward our North Star.

Once all the pieces are in place, fulfillment is possible, but as with everything, it isn't a permanent state. We can sometimes glimpse fulfillment for a moment or maintain it for a month. However, the more we train our brains in purpose and balance, the longer we spend in fulfillment and the easier it is to return to that state.

Crucially, this sense of fulfillment is different from happiness. While there is some overlap, fulfillment is actually a different category of experience from happiness. Aristotle recognized this all the way back in fourth-century-BC Greece. According to him, happiness has two aspects, namely, a "hedonic" aspect that relates to pleasure and a "eudaimonia" aspect (literally, a *good spirit*) that relates to a life well lived. In our terms, happiness relates to the pleasure we get from feeding our impulses. It's an emotion that we feel when a combination of neurotransmitters is released in the brain. Fulfillment is less an emotion than a mood—an overall state of being. We can be fulfilled and happy, but we can also be fulfilled and sad, angry, depressed, or anxious.

This distinction also tracks with what we know about how the brain operates. Happiness, as we've seen already, is driven primarily by dopamine. There's a particular path deep in our brain that regulates our emotions. It extends all the way to our frontal cortex, and it's tied to our memories as well. When we experience a positive stimulus or draw upon the memories that we associate with happiness, our brain releases dopamine. We then try to repeat these behaviors to get the same hit later.

This is our default processing system. It's hardwired in our brains. And it isn't unique to humans. This same pathway is present in many other animals, even if it's less intricate and complex than the one found in humans. Think about it this way: A dog is happy whenever we pet it. It's always happy when we pet it, often regardless of other factors. Because of this, it seeks out these pets every time we are present, looking for any opportunity to achieve this moment of happiness.

Human interaction with the world is obviously far more complex than this. It is nuanced by our memories that allow for more complex connections with other individuals and more intricate relationships to certain behaviors. In other words, in its simplest form, we are designed to find happiness and then seek it again in the same form. But as we know, this leads us into a vicious cycle, constantly craving more intense experiences to achieve the original result. To relive the same level of happiness, we need more dopamine, sending us onto the happiness trajectory that never truly feels fulfilling.

This difficulty in achieving happiness is useful for our species. We struggle with contentment because our chase for dopamine demands that we always seek more: better food, better living conditions, and better romantic partners. This drive for more money and nicer cars is the same drive that pushed us to develop agriculture, found cities, and develop technology. We don't just want to get the same quality of life we're used to; we want to improve life for ourselves and those we care about. This is an essential quality that has allowed our species to rise to the top and dominate every other species on the planet. It's also one of the primary motivators of many religions and life philosophies. Buddhism, Christianity, and modern self-help books all urge us to improve ourselves at every opportunity, to reach some high, almost unattainable ultimate goal.

This same quality eats away at our ability to feel consistently satisfied.

And for good reason: Too much satisfaction, and we would never try to achieve anything. We'd simply sit around, enjoy what we already have, and work the bare minimum to maintain that quality of life. Where would we be as a species, as a society, or as individuals in that case?

Fulfillment is the only answer to this evolutionary dilemma. When we're fulfilled, we level off some of those spikes in dopamine, but we don't then abandon our goals. We don't stop dreaming or enjoying moments of happiness. Instead, fulfillment allows us to train our brains so they don't become flooded with neurotransmitters—whether these neurotransmitters cause happiness, depression, or panic. When we train our brains to reduce these levels, we are actually in a better state to remain focused and achieve our aims, no matter the obstacles we face.

This occurs because reducing the firing of neurotransmitters such as dopamine allows another player in our brain chemistry—namely, endorphins—to better achieve their role. Endorphins dampen stress and discomfort. They give us a sense of calmness and resilience. They cushion our dopamine lows and allow us to feel that sense of long-term well-being we all crave.

We all know the feeling when endorphins are allowed to do their job properly. After a nice meal or a great workout, the positive buzz we have is the result of endorphins. It isn't happiness or joy we're feeling then; it's just a positive state of calmness that lasts for a few hours. We feel less stressed, more relaxed, and generally more easygoing.

This can be our overall state of being if we train our brain for fulfillment. When we break the cycle of dopamine surges by training for purpose and balance, we leave more room for endorphins to do their work. This is an ideal state to be in, both for our own positive mental outlook and for any efforts to achieve our long-term goals.

RECOGNIZING FULFILLMENT

One of the great tragedies in life is that we often realize how good things were only long after the fact. We fail to appreciate the moment while we're living it and only acknowledge the good times once they're past and we're looking back. The same phenomenon can easily happen with fulfillment. We can do everything else right: We can find our purpose and articulate it clearly, we can align that purpose with our work, and we can balance ourselves emotionally while also finding balance in our ambition and perception of time. And we can still miss out on fulfillment simply by failing to recognize it when it occurs.

Because fulfillment is a by-product of purpose and balance, we can access it once at least some of these other elements are in place. But we can become so distracted by the day-to-day demands of life that fulfillment can go completely unacknowledged. Indeed, sometimes, we even convince ourselves that we aren't fulfilled because we're still lacking *something*. Whether it's something material, some internal quality, or some external goal, we think we need just a bit more before we can say we're truly fulfilled. Ironically, this inability to recognize fulfillment can pull us out of the sense of being fulfilled.

And this is a waste of our time because being fulfilled isn't about having everything. It's not about reaching a destination. Remember, it's distinct from dopamine-soaked happiness. Instead, it's about appreciating your sense of direction—whether in the times when you have the wind at your back, a clear sky above, and smooth seas in all directions or in the times when the water is choppy and the skies aflame with lightning. In both cases, so long as you are balanced, purposeful, and sailing toward your North Star, you can be fulfilled.

Once purpose and balance are in place, the key to fulfillment is simply recognizing it whenever we experience it. When we feel a sense of calm and certainty in our direction as we move through life—a sense of contentment with where we've come from and where we're going—we have to label it for what it is. We don't have to wait until we have *everything* in order because we'll never have everything. So long as we're sailing in the right direction and have all the internal resources we need to keep going—so long as we've flattened out those dopamine spikes and turned our focus to our impactful North Star—we can face rough seas or calm waters with equanimity. And that is fulfillment.

This is an energizing mood. Fulfillment isn't about being complacent. Perhaps for some people, fulfillment is possible by just sitting at home and doing as little as possible, but as we covered in the ambition chapter, if you're reading this book, you likely wouldn't enjoy that sort of life. You picked up this book because you want purpose in your work. You want to work and advance in your career while feeling balanced. And you can have that, as well as fulfillment, while feeling as motivated as ever.

In fact, you can feel more motivated. The power of fulfillment is that it doesn't require you to reach a particular milestone. It isn't success dependent. Instead, it's the mood we feel when we are on the right path on a journey we want to be taking. And we can feel that way when things are going well and when new obstacles arise.

But to appreciate its full value, we have to label fulfillment when we experience it—the same way we label purpose.

LOOKING BACK AND LOOKING FORWARD

We can often best recognize fulfillment through our relationship with time. Much of our experience of fulfillment is rooted in memories. Fulfillment rises up in us when we look back at our accomplishments and how we have overcome previous obstacles. There's satisfaction in this look back at the journey so far, and the feeling of fulfillment remains when we consider our mistakes—because those mistakes were part of the journey that led us forward to the present, where we feel purposeful and balanced. In essence, when we cast our minds back down the road we've already traveled, we should feel content and peaceful about the journey so far.

This sense of duration, stability, and satisfaction is a crucial component of fulfillment. It means that fulfillment remains with us across good and bad moments. If we lack this feeling when considering the past, we aren't experiencing fulfillment but rather reliving a dopamine rush from a single success.

Because fulfillment exists over these long spans of time, we can also sense it when we project our outlook forward. We can see the trajectory we are on as it continues to lead further along the road of our career. As we cast our mind in this direction, we should anticipate a prolonged period of balance and purpose, and we should have confidence that it will continue even if we can't see precisely what the future holds for us.

Consider again my daydreams of practicing medicine on a Greek island. It's one of many futures I can imagine in which I feel confident that I will continue to feel purposeful and balanced in my career. The exact nature of the work I do may change dramatically, but I feel a peaceful certainty that I will still be contributing to the world—

making an impact—in a way that accomplishes my purpose. I know I will have the tools to balance my emotions, ambitions, and time commitments professionally, even if I have to switch career paths multiple times in the years ahead.

Time is such a valuable yardstick when measuring fulfillment because it's where purpose and balance sometimes part ways with fulfillment. You can be emotionally balanced and lack a sense of fulfillment when looking back at your accomplishments and struggles. Or you may not feel confident that you can maintain your purpose or balance going forward. If you face a major career change ahead, are you sure your purpose and balance will come with you?

If you're struggling with feeling fulfillment when looking backward or forward, it's likely that this shows some previously unrecognized deficiencies in your purpose or balance. The most likely culprit here is that your purpose is not fully articulated, or you aren't yet living it fully. If you are sure you have found your purpose, then turn to balance. Are you truly feeling balanced emotionally? Have you found the right dynamics around your ambition? Are you appreciating your time effectively?

Run back through all the concepts and brain training we've already covered, and you're likely to find weak points that, once strengthened, can help the pieces click into place, allowing you to find fulfillment across the past, present, and future.

Of course, fulfillment isn't blind to the difficulties of the past or those ahead. When you're at sea, storms are inevitable. Fulfillment allows you to acknowledge that things haven't always been this good and won't always remain this good. You've sailed through some tough times, and tough times are ahead. *This too shall pass*, no matter what you're doing. But when you are fulfilled, you no longer feel upset over previous difficulties or fear those that are ahead.

Remembering those moments and anticipating what's ahead shouldn't rattle your sense of fulfillment, though. If you've found purpose and balance, you know that everything before has led to the present in which those are aligned. And if you've found purpose, balance, and fulfillment once, you can find them again if they're ever lost—as we'll discuss in more detail in chapter 10.

By placing fulfillment on a timeline with the past, present, and future, you can more clearly see that you're on a journey, just like the rest of us. And you now have everything you need to keep moving forward on that journey, no matter what's ahead.

CHAPTER 9

INVESTING IN FULFILLMENT

When I was a teenager, my mom was fond of repeating an old Greek saying: "I wish I had the knowledge I have now when I was younger." She was constantly chiding me for all the time I was throwing away by doing nothing. Like most young people, I felt I had unlimited time to waste on TV, gossip, and just lying around. She would highlight that time wasn't, in fact, infinite. Back then, I didn't get it.

It wasn't the only lesson I couldn't internalize. People close to me would often tell me I needed to learn to control my emotions. In particular, I was hotheaded and excitable in all my decision-making. Every choice was fueled by emotion—and dopamine. I lived almost entirely on impulse. I also struggled with my desire to be recognized for my work and skills. Whether it was tennis, academics, medicine, or the biopharmaceutical industry, I was in endless pursuit of more praise and higher income.

In other words, while I had my purpose in place from a young age, I was completely unbalanced in my emotions, ambition, and use of time. To avoid making the necessary changes, I would try to rationalize my behavior, but all I had to offer were paper-thin excuses.

I wish I could say the reason I started down the fulfillment trajectory was because of the ideas in this book, but those came later. Instead, as I got older, experience naturally cooled me down a bit. I began to slow down and take emotion out of my thought process. This is a progression most of us go through as a by-product of aging. Our experiences create memories, and those memories rewire our brains. We often refer to this process as gaining wisdom.

However, that's not to say that the principles in this book played no part in my own journey. I may have started to improve my temper, balance my ambitions, and appreciate time, but the brain training recommended in this book accelerated my access to wisdom. Instead of slowly realizing my mistakes, I absorbed the lessons in my thirties and forties, when I was still young enough and early enough in my career that I could really use the information.

As I really dug in and did the work, I began to see clearly that it was pointless to fervently pursue recognition at the expense of more impactful goals that could improve the world around me. After all, impact often outlasts recognition. Who is the most recognized figure in the world? There are a few candidates, but near the top is the pope. But who was the pope seventy years ago? Unless you're a devout Catholic, you probably don't know.

It's a fool's errand to build a career around the desire for recognition at the expense of purpose, balance, and fulfillment. It's also foolish to waste time when we have so little of it in the first place—or to make rash, emotional decisions that may feel good at the time but tend to lead to poor choices with long-term consequences.

It was in my late thirties that for the first time, I could see how my behavior had limited my professional life. I may have been successful so far, but in all that success, I had rarely felt professionally fulfilled. Luckily, that changed once I started training my brain using the strategies I've laid out in this book.

I saw similar improvements at home. With renewed purpose, I was able to become the anchor of my family. With emotional balance, I could listen more, help more, and provide stability and calm. This enriched my family life immensely. My family has highlighted just how much I changed over the period I was developing these skills. I became less reactive. I was a lot less binary in my decision-making. I became more accepting and learned the value of conversation and curiosity when interacting with each of my family members.

I did all of this without compromising any of my personal beliefs. I'm a better husband, father, son, and friend, just as I'm a better doctor, researcher, and leader.

ACHIEVING FULFILLMENT THROUGHOUT LIFE

The purpose of this book is to help you gain the wisdom we've discussed as early as possible. Instead of needing to reach the age of sixty to rewire your brain through experience, you can do so at twenty-five or forty. This can allow you to find purpose in your work earlier in your career. You can achieve balance while you're still in the stressful years of professional growth. And you can feel fulfilled across entire decades instead of looking back at the end of your professional life and regretting that it's too late to experience contentment.

But this is only really one half of the value of the ideas we've covered. In chapter 2, I explained that we really have two parallel purposes. We have focused on one of those in these pages—our professional purpose—but our personal purpose is at least equally as important. In fact, our brains would argue that these aren't different purposes at all but two aspects of one. While we experience work life and home life as separate components of our existence, this is a misunderstanding that comes from how we organize time in modern life. Taking care of your mental health is a crucial step in achieving fulfillment. If you don't have wellness within yourself, you are unlikely to be able to develop or improve other aspects of your life. You can't pour from an empty pot. These days, work and home are two separate places with distinct responsibilities—although that has been changing with the increase in remote work positions. In the past, when everyone was a farmer or a hunter-gatherer, this separation did not exist, and our brain still doesn't really register a divide here. The brain is a single organ. It doesn't dedicate one hemisphere to work life and another to home life. Instead, it experiences life holistically. If we are stressed at home, that stress remains with us at work. If we're depressed about our career, we feel depressed on the weekends, wasting our precious time being absorbed in negative feelings rather than enjoying our family.

Likewise, positive alignment in one area of life feeds into the other. If I have purpose in my life as a father and husband, I feel more purposeful in my work, even if I don't like the job I have. If I cultivate emotional balance in my interactions at the office, I can call upon that same balance when one of my kids accidentally breaks a window.

So once we have alignment between our purpose, balance, and fulfillment at work, the next natural step is to pursue it in our personal lives. Or, to coin a phrase, we have to expand these techniques across the rest of life in order to achieve "holistic fulfillment."

Luckily, once we achieve professional fulfillment, we are far closer to achieving fulfillment in our personal life. The reason is simple: Many of the same techniques and principles we've covered for professional purpose, balance, and fulfillment also apply to our personal lives.

For instance, I became a better listener at home once I learned to listen to feedback and criticism at work. It's not just anger management either. If you struggle to use your time wisely when you're at home, you can slow down and really appreciate it in the same way you do at work. If you feel purposeless outside of the office, the same tools for finding purpose at work will work at home.

Remember, it's all one brain. There is no personal brain and professional brain. So, the training you've done in one area will work in the other, so long as you consciously employ the same strategies.

COMMITTING TO CONTINUOUS CURIOSITY

Achieving the wisdom of fulfillment is a great gift, and the earlier we can acquire it—professionally and personally—the better. But we have to remember that this is not the kind of wisdom we can learn, implement, and then forget. Like purpose and balance, fulfillment is not something we achieve once and then move on from. It's something that we cultivate and develop forever. And a huge part of that maintenance is simply committing to continuing to proactively explore ourselves and the world around us.

I started this book with a call to be curious. We have to be curious about ourselves, others, our interests and talents, and outside perspectives on those qualities in order to find our purpose. Just because we have a purpose now doesn't mean we should shut down that drive.

In fact, though I haven't drawn as much attention to it, that curiosity has been running through this book ever since the beginning. So much of training our brain for balance involves a desire to slow down and ask the right questions. Fulfillment requires the curiosity to look around and recognize when we feel calm, certain, purposeful, and balanced.

We should continue this practice forever. We need to ask questions about not only our purpose, balance, and fulfillment but also about everything else in the world. We should encourage our curiosity about how a car engine works. We should cultivate our curiosity about the people around us. What are their interests? What is their purpose? How do they see us?

We can extend this curiosity to the tools we use. For instance, we should continue to explore technology and consider how it can help us achieve our purpose—all while remaining curious about how that technology affects us.

And we should remain curious about time. We have to remember not just to slow down and take our time but also to appreciate that time. Are we remaining aware of the time we're using? Are we using that time well? Are we taking the time to find new experiences? Again, there is a huge benefit to this kind of curiosity beyond purpose and balance: Appreciation of time expands our sense of time. We can increase how long we feel we're living simply by thinking about it more often and more deeply.

When we are children, time seems endless. Part of the reason for this is that, during childhood, we are still forming our sense of time. But the other part is that, as children, we are constantly encountering new experiences and forming new memories. This is how our brains judge how much time has passed. As we get older, we pursue fewer unique experiences, so time feels like it is speeding up.

If we are curious and appreciate our time, we create more memories, and it feels like time slows down. The best way to extend our life is to alter our perception of time, and the best way to do that is by being present and fulfilled and remaining curious.

As we pursue this curiosity, we should be willing to act upon what we learn. This includes revisiting purpose, balance, and fulfillment (as we'll discuss further in the chapter), but it should also include other aspects of life. If we find that some form of technology is negatively affecting our lives, we should change our behavior. If we find some new aspect of our work more interesting than our current responsibilities, we should see if our purpose aligns with that change. And remember, the best way to extend our lives is to alter our perception of time—which we can do all the better when we're able to be present, fulfilled, and curious.

And as we prepare to act, we should do so with a willingness to make big changes in our lives. We shouldn't do this flippantly or without balanced and careful thought, of course, but sometimes, a big swing is the right one. This is, after all, how I went from a career as a university professor to working in the pharmaceutical industry. It's also how I leaped into running my own company. Once it was clear that I felt this was the direction best suited for my purpose, I took a big step instead of half measures. And each time, it was the right call.

If you think through your current situation and you need a big change, don't avoid it for fear of risking your purpose. Perhaps you need to make a big change in order to further evolve your purpose. If everything else aligns, take the plunge.

FINDING COMMUNITY

One of the best ways we can maintain our curiosity, as well as our purpose, balance, and fulfillment, is by finding others who can encourage these qualities within us and help us further cultivate them.

Humans are social beings. We crave connection, and connection feeds our positive behaviors. And we can enter a virtuous cycle of positive reinforcement that helps us evolve our purpose, improve our balance, and remain connected to our fulfillment—all thanks to the curiosity we experience through connection.

This is more possible now because fulfillment actually makes us more receptive to feedback and advice. We can afford to be more giving and understanding because we feel we have the extra resources to do so. Our holistic sense of fulfillment makes us more generous with others. We're more open and more willing to give them our time and attention.

Fulfillment naturally radiates interest outward. Purpose already has a natural, externally facing altruistic side, and now that we also feel balanced and confident in our ability to maintain both principles, we can shift that genuine interest in others so that we focus on genuine curiosity about them—their feelings, their opinions, and their experiences. Fulfillment makes it easier to give back what we expect from others—whether that's honesty, support, or an unbiased opinion.

All of this has positive knock-on benefits for us as individuals and within our communities. For instance, because we can engage with others through more genuine curiosity, we can better understand their behaviors and choices without judgment, allowing us to learn from their experiences and grow closer to them.

This isn't the case before we're fulfilled. When we lack fulfillment, we're constantly in troubleshooting mode. We're so tied up in our exhausting swing from emotional highs to emotional lows and so ground down by a lack of purpose that we struggle to remain receptive to others' needs and wants. During such periods, connection is dependent on how we're feeling at a particular moment. If we're in the midst of en emotional rush after a career success, we can be convivial and open during that dopamine high. After our dopamine crash, we shut down.

Fulfillment changes all that by opening us up to new experiences and relationships. Because we've fit the pieces of the puzzle together in a pattern that works for our brain, we're able to create new pathways with the right circuits firing at the right time.

Fulfillment unlocks so much because it changes how our brain's biochemistry works. There are three major neurotransmitters that positively affect our mood. We've covered two of them—dopamine and serotonin—as well as the endorphins that stabilize us and give us balance. The third neurotransmitter is oxytocin. This is sometimes referred to as the love hormone. It's the hormone of trust, social bonding, and emotional connection.

When we have more oxytocin in our system, we are more capable of building strong social connections. And as with endorphins, when we aren't constantly pumping our heads full of dopamine, we can produce more of that oxytocin. And that creates room for more and deeper connections.

These new connections are valuable on multiple levels. They allow us to practice curiosity and learn new things. Through our new experiences, we also strengthen our sense of purpose and find new ways to maintain balance or appreciate fulfillment. And there's also professional value in this behavior. If you want to be successful, you have to care about other people, and fulfillment helps you get there. We train our brains to have positive external focus, and that allows us to build deeper relationships—the kind we need within the company we work at and when we are considering taking our career in a new direction.

Fundamentally, we need these new connections on a very practical level because we need the help of others if we want to achieve anything. The truth is that no one can teach themselves everything. We rely on our social connections to supplement our understanding and introduce new ideas. I could never develop a biotech treatment by myself. I need others who understand the complexities of a treatment and the aspects of the development process that I am only vaguely familiar with. I need outside perspectives to help me see the obstacles I encounter in a new light.

And we need such resources in every kind of work and in our personal lives. None of us are lone wolves. We all require a pack. One human, isolated, will never achieve what multiple individuals can achieve together. This is true even of most of the great artists we think of as isolated geniuses. Most of them actually actively interacted with others in their communities.

Our community can offer new ideas. It can also offer emotional support. When we're out of balance and lack purpose, we can feel very isolated. But as we develop our community in moments of fulfillment, we can see clearly that we are not alone. Everyone is on their own odyssey, seeking purpose, balance, and fulfillment. We can learn from those who are at a different place in this process, and we can encourage one another as we go.

Even Odysseus needs his fair share of oxytocin-fueled community bonding. Odysseus may be the hero of *The Odyssey*, but he doesn't make it home on his own. All along the way, he requires the help of others. When he washes ashore after a shipwreck, he only survives because of the help of the Phaeacians. When he returns to Ithaca, he finds shelter at the home of his old friend, Eumaeus the swineherd. His son, Telemachus, helps him defeat the suitors who would otherwise kill him.

The Odyssey is, in many ways, the story of a lonely journey, but even there, we can see dozens of characters who help Odysseus on his quest.

Ultimately, the more we can merge our curiosity and internal journey with the perspectives we receive from others—whether those are direct comments, vague allusions, or even just body language—the deeper and more long-lasting we can make our fulfillment. The closer we align our internal perception with our external perception, the better we can perform in the workplace and maintain purpose, balance, and fulfillment across our whole lives.

As we seek out our own community and support structures, we should consciously open ourselves up and be receptive to incoming information. When forming our purpose, we have to expose ourselves to the thoughts and opinions of others. That is the only way we can get an outside perspective on who we are and what we are good at. We can take this same spirit of openness further now, showing curiosity about the purpose of others while still receiving feedback on how those others perceive our actions and choices.

We all need a reality check from time to time. It's easy to get trapped in our own internal perception and lose track of how we present ourselves to others. Fulfillment can make us complacent. Everything is going well enough, and we feel good enough, so we can start letting purpose and balance slide. Showing curiosity to our community can give us a chance to look in the mirror and see ourselves from a different perspective.

We still need to maintain our filters. We decide what we internalize, what we hold on to, and what we discard. But a trained brain, by default, recognizes and sorts incoming information better than an untrained brain that's always on the hunt for dopamine.

DON'T WAIT

I was able to salvage fulfillment in my career and strengthen my relationships with my family because I developed the wisdom of fulfillment early enough to use it. If I had waited for this wisdom to come naturally, it might not have really sunk in until I was a lonely, disappointed man in my sixties or seventies. By then, my career would have been almost entirely over—with many bridges burned and opportunities missed. My relationships with family and friends might have been permanently ruined.

I'm deeply grateful that I did the work early enough to find fulfillment while I can make the most of it. I hope the same can be true for you. But to ensure that's the case, you have to get working on training your brain now.

Many of us come by some of the lessons in this book naturally at various points along our professional odyssey. We end up training our brain through experience—learning from times when we allowed our ambitions to grow too great or when we spent years aimlessly working without purpose—and perhaps we're lucky enough to put all of the pieces together at some point without consciously working on the process. But if we leave everything to nature and experience, we risk this wisdom coming too late.

Life is simply better the sooner we achieve these qualities. We are more content. Our relationships are stronger. And we achieve more in our work. We're all on a lifelong odyssey, so we may as well set ourselves up to sail with as much comfort, confidence, and contentment as possible—and do it as soon as possible.

CHAPTER 10

A LIFELONG ODYSSEY

The most frustrating obstacles we face are the ones that are beyond our control. Along with the exasperation we feel from the difficulty itself, there's a sense of helplessness when we realize there's little we can do to change our circumstances. When we lose our job because the company is downsizing or see a promotion go to an undeserving colleague because of nepotism, it stings more than if we had done something wrong ourselves.

It's nice to imagine that some technique or philosophical principle could give us more control over our destiny, but the reality is that sometimes, life just happens to us, and all we can do is react. I've had jobs in which I felt purposeful, balanced, and fulfilled. I was doing great work that would have a real impact on people. I was well regarded by others in the company and had every reason to think I'd continue moving up the organizational chart into a leadership position. Then, the circumstances of my position would change.

Through no fault of my own, I would find myself forced by outside events to make a change.

This happened when I was working at Pfizer, the first biopharmaceutical company I worked for in which I really felt balanced. As you might recall from chapter 6, in my first two companies in this field, I'd been overly ambitious and had struggled with emotional balance. By the time I moved back to Boston from Los Angeles, I'd finally trained my brain to allow me to succeed in this area. I felt rejuvenated, newly purposeful, fully balanced, and fulfilled in every aspect of the work.

Then, everything was turned upside down when the company made a major pivot. The leadership looked at the numbers and decided to exit neuroscience drug development entirely. They just didn't see any profit in it in the long term. Whether they were right or wrong is irrelevant. Again, this had nothing to do with me or my work. There was nothing I could have done to change the minds of the board and executive team. All I could do was attempt to adapt to these new circumstances.

As the team broke up, some found jobs elsewhere in the company, but like the majority, I decided to move on. The loss of my position was naturally unbalancing at a time when I'd finally secured that balance. My ambitions pulled in different directions, and I had to ask whether this was really a field in which I could best employ my purpose. Was there any other work in the medical field that I could focus on that would be less chaotic?

But because I'd already found fulfillment in my work—as well as purpose and balance—I knew how to get my bearings back quickly. I took the lessons I could from the experience and got to work revisiting my purpose, reestablishing my balance, and uniting both behind fulfillment as I went in search of a new position.

Interrogating my purpose once more, I realized that I wanted to stick with the neuroscience field. I was offered the chance to work on drug trials to reduce obesity, but I turned it down. This time, it wasn't because my unbalanced ambitions made me afraid to work in an area outside my expertise. I simply knew that my purpose was still drawing me toward developing neuropsychiatric treatments.

Reestablishing my footing in purpose, balance, and fulfillment, I decided to go to a company called Teva, a large corporation that was just entering the neuroscience space. I became part of a team that allowed me to engage in the process of actually getting a drug or treatment approved. It was even more rewarding than my job at Pfizer.

But this job had its own complications. My family was settled in Boston, while the job was in Philadelphia. After uprooting them to California only to bring them back to Boston, I couldn't justify another move. This threw my time balance completely out of whack, as well as my personal purpose. Every week, I flew down to Philly on Sunday evening and flew back home on Friday evening. My kids were young at the time, and leaving them for the week was always painful. So while I was balanced in my work, my personal life was suffering.

Despite my best efforts and immense sacrifice on the part of my family, this job was also a failure. Once again, I recognized there was nothing I could do to change the situation. I couldn't change my commute or how well the company did. All I could do was learn whatever lessons I could from the experience and use my purpose, balance, and fulfillment to guide my next choice.

That's exactly what I did. In 2017, I decided to stop looking for opportunities at large pharmaceutical companies. Instead, I went to a smaller company, realizing I could potentially find more consistency and control there. I brought everything I'd learned in the industry to that job, as well as balance, purpose, and fulfillment.

I've continued on this path ever since. I've worked for, built, and consulted with smaller companies to help them grow. Obviously, I still only have so much control over everything that happens in my career and my life. I've already mentioned the loss of certain grants that occurred while writing this book. Such obstacles will continue to arise from time to time. And I'm sure there will come a day when events force me to make a bigger change again. That's just the nature of life. Some event will inevitably knock a bit of purpose, balance, or fulfillment out of my sails. Luckily, I know how to repair them and keep sailing on.

This is how it is to be on a lifelong odyssey. We're all out here sailing on the seas, heading toward our own individual North Star, and we have no control over the weather. No matter how much we try to chart a journey under clear skies, the longer we're on the water, the more likely we'll run into a bad storm. But that's OK. We just have to accept that part of our journey is about rediscovery. It's about reassessing and reinventing our purpose, balance, and fulfillment—from now until our journey is truly over.

GET AS CLOSE TO FULFILLMENT AS POSSIBLE

I recognize that some of the examples in this book are probably a bit idealized. I know that it isn't always possible to uproot your life and directly pursue purpose the way I have at times. I've been lucky that my purpose aligns so perfectly with a prominent career with many opportunities. That isn't the case for everyone.

At the same time, balance isn't always as straightforward for some people. Some have to contend with mental health concerns that limit their ability to regulate certain emotions. There may also be demands on their time that they can't adjust—a sick family member they have to attend to, for instance.

However, none of that should discount the advice I've shared. Instead, we should see purpose, balance, and fulfillment as a sort of North Star in their own right. While it is definitely possible to attain all three principles, at times, we have to see them as somewhat aspirational. In such moments, our aim is to get as close to them as possible.

Consider purpose. If you work on Wall Street but feel your purpose would be best lived painting watercolors in Paris, such a radical change isn't always possible. But if you recognize that the job of painting watercolors isn't actually your purpose, you can take steps to move closer to the deeper purpose within. Strip away the idealized dream, and you can consider what it is within that idea that suggests purpose to you.

Why do you want to paint? Do you want to convey a message through your creative work? Do you enjoy connecting with people through your creativity? Do you relish the opportunity to communicate deeper emotions to others?

Once you have a concrete sense of that deeper purpose—which, remember, is always altruistic and external looking—is there another way to achieve it that is less dramatic and allows you to maintain the life you've already built?

Sometimes, there's a perfect alignment here. There may be a position as head of finance at a museum or an opportunity to become a professor of economics in a bustling artistic college town. But even if such opportunities aren't available, your aim should be to get as close to your purpose as possible. Find a job that gets you closest to that purpose for now, and you can continue to seek a better fit.

The alternative is to delay the process of achieving balance and fulfilment. You won't be able to truly enjoy your career because you'll be trapped on the happiness trajectory, leaping from one dopamine high to the next and trying to avoid the huge drops while ignoring the lack of fulfillment you feel in your work.

The same is true of balance. Perfect balance is not always available in every moment in life. I've been through a bad divorce. I was not emotionally balanced at that time. Nor was my time balanced when I was commuting to Philadelphia. But even in such tough moments, we have to remain conscious of the imbalance and wrestle with it, getting as close to balance as we can.

What this book hopes to achieve is to show you the path you can follow to find these core principles within yourself. But this isn't the sort of path we walk down once and arrive at a final destination. It's a path we walk over and over again throughout our lives. Sometimes, we can get all the way to the goal at the end, and we can rest for a while before walking the path again. At other times, we can only walk as far down it as our current circumstances allow us. Each time we walk down this path, we have to be willing to ask ourselves the same tough questions and investigate them with curiosity. Do we still feel purposeful in the same way as we did last year? If our purpose has changed, should we consider a change in our career? Is there anything else we could be doing?

As we train our brain, we should think of it like training a muscle. The more you work it, the stronger it gets. But if you spend too long away from the gym, all the benefits can fade away.

That's why the true value of this whole process is the method itself—the means of finding the answers—more than the act of successfully achieving purpose or balance at one point or another in life. It's the *process* of bringing these ideas to a conscious level, thinking through your purpose, training your brain for balance, and recognizing fulfillment. It's the journey, not the destination.

Because no matter what we do, we will lose purpose or balance at times. We'll wake up and realize we aren't as fulfilled as we once were. But if we stick with the method, we can always find our way back to these principles. And the more we train our brains, the more we'll be able to manage these situations effectively, no matter the adversity we face.

FINDING YOUR WAY BACK TO PURPOSE

As we already know, purpose is never meant to remain static. It's a living part of who we are, and it changes as we change. Think of it as a living breathing "thing" that always needs nutrients to evolve and grow. The best way to avoid losing purpose, then, is to keep redefining and evolving it as we develop professionally. As we gaze within, we have to be honest and true to ourselves, even if the consequences require us to make a significant change in our career. It's possible to be in a good job, making good money, and find that our purpose has left that position behind. To ignore that change only puts more distance between us and our purpose.

If we've really done this internal work and trained our brains to regularly reevaluate our purpose, it should remain rock solid enough that it stays with us and evolves over time. However, there are times we can still lose purpose. This most often happens when life serves us situations that are so intense that they shake up the very foundation of who we are. Most commonly, this occurs when we have children. Before having a family, most people are intensely focused on their profession. Their professional purpose likely reflects their level of ambition. But all of this can shift radically once a child enters their life. At that moment, professional purpose may either take a back seat or completely change direction.

This happened with my wife. Prior to starting a family, her purpose revolved around being a lawyer. She was dedicated to pursuing justice for her clients and advancing at her law firm. Once she had kids, her purpose shifted. Being a lawyer still had some theoretical value, but it was dwarfed by her personal purpose to be a stay-at-home mom.

But this isn't the only time purpose can take a huge, unexpected turn. When someone has been seriously ill, lost a loved one, or been through an intense negative economic experience, purpose sometimes changes in unpredictable ways.

This shift can be jarring—particularly if your purpose wasn't firmly in place before—but thankfully, the solution is straightforward. If you feel you've lost purpose, start by doing a little investigating. Did you truly lose purpose, or is this a temporary state? Are you just burned out? Are you discouraged?

If you're fairly certain that you have lost your purpose, simply go back to part I and run through the whole process again. No skipping steps.

Again, though, we should be comfortable doing this anyway, even if we're only evolving our purpose. We should regularly cycle through all these steps, and the more we do so, the more we train our brains to do it automatically. Once our brains do this without prompting, we can shift and adjust our purpose fairly easily, and we'll notice quickly if it has undergone a major transformation.

RECOVERING YOUR BALANCE

Unlike purpose, which we should generally be able to evolve and adapt as we go (barring those really big life changes), it's far more likely we'll lose one form of balance or another from time to time just with the normal shifts in life. I've already mentioned a few times in this chapter that this has happened to me. I lost balance when I was going through a divorce. At the time, I was in my first CEO role, and the strain of that event, combined with a new level of pressure I wasn't used to, deeply affected my personal and professional life, as was very clear for all to see.

For me, and I think in general, the best course of action in such moments is to be open to advice and seek out counsel from trusted sources. This advice should come in two forms: advice for daily decision-making and advice on reestablishing balance.

In regard to the former, when we are too unbalanced to make wise decisions, the wisest course is to let someone else think clearly for us until we can bring ourselves back into balance. This can free up the mental and emotional space to rediscover our balance.

If you do seek out advice from others, remember not to go to just one person. Choose at least three people and let them help you think through your situation. They can be friends, family members, mentors, or therapists. I know many people who have gone to a combination of all of them in periods of imbalance.

Personally, I sought out professional coaches. At the time, I was too proud to admit I was struggling professionally to those who were close to me because my whole identity hinged on my professional purpose, so I went to those outside my circle who could help me think and adjust to my new reality.

Again, such moments of imbalance are inevitable. There will come a time when your ambition is out of balance, perhaps when a big promotion is on the line. Your time can be unbalanced when you become obsessed with a particular deliverable. Or you'll experience emotional imbalance after a major setback that you can't seem to get over.

These are all natural occurrences in a career. But if you've trained your brain, you should be able to recognize these moments of imbalance quickly. And so long as you recognize when this is happening, you can reach out to those who can help until you ride out the spikes in your neurotransmitters and regain balance.

AN ENDLESS ODYSSEY

The Odyssey would be a pretty boring story if it was just five hundred pages of Odysseus slowly making his way back to Ithaca with a single, clear purpose permanently in mind. Homer certainly recognized this. Instead of telling such a straightforward tale, Homer described Odysseus constantly failing in his purpose and balance. Odysseus falls in love more than once on his way back home. He becomes distracted for long periods. In fact, we meet him at the beginning of the narrative after wasting years on an island with a nymph named Calypso. Talk about a lack of appreciation for time.

Odysseus makes big mistakes over and over again. At one point, he loses all emotional balance and mocks the Cyclops Polyphemus after he thinks he's bested the giant monster. This moment of hubris leads to Poseidon, the father of Polyphemus, cursing Odysseus, which further delays Odysseus and causes him even more heartache than he's already experienced.

But Odysseus recovers from such moments because he's so aware of himself. When he realizes he's lingered too long on the island with Calypso, he laments and refocuses on his ultimate purpose. And when he is about to pass the island of the Sirens—mythical creatures that are half bird and half woman, whose song hypnotizes men and causes them to turn their ships toward an island where they will crash and be devoured—he knows that he will be even more susceptible than most.

After all, he's been through several episodes that distracted him from his purpose already. So, as he passes the island, he ties himself to the stern of his ship and has his crew put beeswax in their ears. He sees potential imbalance and lost purpose, and he adjusts to it.

We would all do well to take a page from Odysseus here, especially since our odyssey, unlike his, has no real end. Instead, we will be at the sea for the rest of our professional lives, sailing toward that North Star we'll never actually reach. As we sail along, our purpose will change. In ten years, our balance will be different from what it is today. Fulfillment will evolve over time as well. But so long as we hold on to the techniques in this book, we can always find our way back to our course again.

Δ

CONCLUSION

I'm not the first person to connect Odysseus to the professional or personal journey we all take in life. There's a tradition of similar metaphors that goes back to ancient Greece itself. The great modern Greek poet, C. P. Cavafy, continued this long tradition and wrote stirringly about Odysseus's journey back to Ithaca. As we end this part of the journey that we've shared together, I think it's worth sharing his words, which I've loosely translated:

As you set sail for the island of Ithaka
hope your sail is a long one,
full of adventure, full of discovery.
Laistrygonians, Cyclops,
angry Poseidon—don't be afraid of them:
you'll never encounter them on your way
as long as you keep your spirits high,
as long as a rare excitement
stirs your mind and your body.

You won't encounter them
unless you carry them inside your soul.

We all hope to have a long journey ahead of us. And if we do, the message of this book is that you can determine whether the obstacles you face in your career turn into Poseidons and Cyclopses or whether you pass by them like a minor storm at sea. If you choose to follow the ideas we've covered in the ten chapters you've just read, you can train your brain to reduce these gods and monsters to interruptions in an odyssey leading toward your ultimate impactful purpose. You have the power to maintain balance even as you skim over choppy surf and to sail forth with a heart full of fulfillment.

Since that's on offer, there's really no reason to wait any longer. There's no harm in starting to train your brain now. There's no downside. It won't hurt your career or your family life. Far from it, in fact. Training your brain can only have a positive impact across every aspect of your life. Even just incorporating a few of the ideas can improve your quality of life. For instance, imagine how much more work you could accomplish if you trained your brain to appreciate time better. Imagine how much more quality time you could spend with your family. Training your brain for time, in fact, gives you more subjective time. Life feels longer and fuller.

None of these ideas will reduce the importance, value, or pleasure you gain from achieving your dreams and indulging your impulses. You don't have to forego happiness or joy. These are all still very valuable tools. They just stop overwhelming your decisions and actions. They don't limit your ability to pursue money, power, or fame; they simply allow you to keep these impulses in their proper place in your life. You prevent them from leading you down the wrong path or facing major emotional setbacks when you fall short when attempting to achieve one of your ambitions.

Listen—I like fast cars. I still drive one. I like making money and being appreciated. But these are no longer the central motivations behind my work or pivotal to how I understand my life. And my life is infinitely better for it. I can handle the difficulties that come my way professionally, and in my personal life, I'm more present as a father, husband, son, and friend.

There's one final reason not to delay implementing these principles in your life: This process will take time. There will be benefits from a little training, but real results will take consistency and effort over a longer period. You won't find purpose in an afternoon, and you can't rewire your brain overnight. Training your brain for balance takes consistent effort. The more you pursue these principles, the more benefits you'll see, but you have to pursue them consistently over time before they become automatic.

The sooner you start, the sooner you'll be swimming in the warm seas of fulfillment. And the benefits may be unexpected. Several times in this book, I've mentioned my dream of becoming a doctor on a Greek island. This past spring, I made it a (temporary) reality. I volunteered to visit five islands over a single week. I saw about one hundred neurology patients in that period. It was exhausting work, but I felt deeply fulfilled throughout and afterward. That was time well spent.

You now have all you need to achieve purpose, balance, and fulfillment—professionally and personally.

And with that, I wish you happy travels. Or in the words of Cavafy:

Keep the island of Ithaka always in your mind.
Arriving there is what you're destined for.
But, by no means, don't rush your journey in any way.
Better if it lasts for years,
so you're older by the time you reach the island,
wealthy with all the experience you've gained on the way,
not expecting Ithaka to make you rich.

Δ

ACKNOWLEDGMENTS

To everyone who believed in me or not—you all helped me become a better version of me.

ABOUT THE AUTHOR

Dr. Spyros (Spyropanos) Papapetropoulos is a board-certified neurologist, neuroscientist, and biopharmaceutical CEO whose career bridges hard science, entrepreneurship, and human-centered leadership. Born in Athens, Greece, in 1972 and later forging his path in the United States, he has served as a professor at the University of Miami Leonard M. Miller School of Medicine and as a consultant in neurology at Massachusetts General Hospital. His scientific résumé includes more than two hundred peer-reviewed papers, book chapters, books, and patents, along with pivotal contributions to several FDA-approved therapies.

Yet it is Dr. Papapetropoulos's fascination with people—as much as with neurons—that powers this book. After witnessing both exemplary and toxic workplace cultures, he spent years documenting what truly elevates modern-day professionals. Those notes evolved into a practical framework for transforming the way one approaches day-to-day professional highs and lows, blending insights from neuroscience, mental health advocacy, and real-world executive experience.

Today, Dr. Papapetropoulos leads a fast-growing biotech company focused on developing novel treatments for stress and anxiety disorders, mentors emerging entrepreneurs, and champions initiatives that broaden awareness of workplace mental health issues. A proud father of four, devoted dog lover, and perennial tennis hopeful, he remains anchored by his Greek heritage and grateful for the opportunities he has found in the United States. His guiding belief—*knowledge is a lifelong journey*—continues to drive his curiosity, his commitment to people, and his mission to build workplaces where both brains and hearts can thrive.

www.ingramcontent.com/pod-product-compliance
Lightning Source LLC
LaVergne TN
LVHW050550120926
847757LV00002B/32
9798891882461